BACK to JERUSALEM

the 30 Day Devotional

BACK to JERUSALEM

the 30 Day Devotional

by Eugene Bach

PREFACE

In the next 30 days you will hear the voices of Chinese believers who have been beaten, tortured, and thrown into prison for the gospel of Jesus Christ. Some of the individuals whose voices echo in these daily devotions are no longer living, but their messages help put the focus back on Jesus Christ and to share with us His heart for the lost.

As you listen to these voices, please set aside everything you think you know about following Christ and ask yourself some very simple questions on a daily basis, questions like, "Why is China experiencing the largest revival in the history of the world, with an estimated one million people per month coming to Christ, even though it is a Communist country?" and, "Why are the wealthiest, most evangelized Christian countries not reaching the poorest, most unevangelized countries in the world?" or, if you must, "Why did I spend $19.95 on this book?"

Respected theologians might not all agree with the ideas and teachings regarding suffering that are contained in this devotional, but armchair Christians in the West can learn many things from the believers in China today.

The Chinese have a vision to raise up 100,000 missionaries who will be sent out to every tribe, nation, and tongue between the borders of China and Jerusalem. This is bound to be one of the largest coordinated mission movements in history and it is called Back to Jerusalem.

Back to Jerusalem is the vision of the Chinese church to leave China, follow the old trade routes of the Silk Road, and take the gospel to the most dangerous and unreached people groups in the world today.

The course for missiology in theological seminaries is being re-written by the illegal underground house church movement in China. China has been experiencing the world's largest revival for several decades and now the Christians in China are hungry to take the gospel into other countries around the world.

As the number of Christians in China continues to rise, the number of missionaries sent to other 'closed' countries that do not welcome Christians is also growing. Today, the estimated number of Christians in China is predicted to be anywhere between 130 to 150 million believers. Because of the lack of transparency in China, it is not easy to find an exact figure that everyone can agree upon. However, one thing that is abundantly clear is that this massive church is growing at a breakneck speed. A common estimate is that there are more than 30,000 new believers in China coming to Christ every day! Whatever the real numbers may be, one thing is quite certain—China is experiencing the world's largest revival.

As the Chinese church experiences explosive numerical growth, it also takes its increasing spiritual responsibility very seriously. Something worth noting is that the explosive growth IS NOT taking place equally within the official government church and its underground counterpart. The number of new believers within the house churches in China is growing exponentially on a daily basis, as are their Bible schools, missionary schools, and outreach programs. They are also raising up an army of young people who have the passion and vision to take the gospel into the far reaches of China as well as the area between China and Jerusalem that is often referred to as the 10/40 Window. This army of young people is ready to lay down their lives to preach the gospel in countries that are openly hostile to evangelism.

The Back to Jerusalem vision of the Chinese house church is not some whimsical 'pipedream' but a reality. Missionaries are at this very moment leaving China for some of the most dangerous countries on earth, and they are not going as renowned preachers and evangelists, as you will read in their messages for this daily devotional. They are going as businessmen, workers, and students, ready to work for little pay, live in the worst areas, and abandon everything for the sake of the gospel.

This movement of missionaries from China has the potential to become the largest recorded number of missionaries from one country at one time in the history of the church, and it will not happen by accident. The Back to Jerusalem vision, to preach the gospel to all the world, including the 10/40 Window, will happen deliberately and systematically, but perhaps not with a methodology that appears normal to the western observer. The Church in the West has been programmed to expect missions movements to be built around denominations or personalities, and to include headquarters, control mechanisms, centralized authority, and often a fair amount of media-driven hype. Yet, none of these characteristics would accurately depict what is taking place within the Chinese house church.

The evangelistic effort by Chinese house church missionaries is taking place in the business world, in classrooms, and in harvest fields with very limited reporting of outcomes, very little (if any) funding, and very little control from a centralized authority—and it is confounding Western theological academia.

You see, Back to Jerusalem is not the name of an organization per se, but that of a vision. It is the call of God to evangelize the most unreached people groups in the world and, as such, CANNOT be owned by any denomination, organization, church, or personality. It is shared by charismatic and more conservative Christians alike, and is carried out by the underground house church as well as some in the official state church of China. It is not controlled by any one group or owned by a singular personality. Back to Jerusalem was ignited by God, is sustained at His pleasure, and cannot be contained by any geographical borders. It is the Chinese version of the Great Commission, or as some would say, "It is the Great Commission with Kung-Pao flavor."

Back to Jerusalem (BTJ) is a concept that exists outside the western drama of separation of Church and State because the Chinese underground house church has never produced a dichotomy between their secular and spiritual life. Concepts that separate Christ from any part of the life of the Christian experience have not yet been adopted by Chinese Christians. For the Chinese believer, church is a body of believers that assembles in homes, caves, or even prison cells. The Chinese understanding of the Bible has not defined God as a being who can be maintained in harsh rigid structures poorly constructed by the hands of feeble man. The liberty of the Lord is without limits and no building is able to contain Him, and, more importantly, no building is able to keep Him out. God exists in all things pertaining to the life of man: business, relationships, politics—everything.

For Christians in the West to understand the Chinese underground house church and its teachings within this 30-day devotional, it is important that these barriers, if not completely removed, are at least challenged. God, business, people, education, political beliefs, home, and even seemingly more trivial matters such as choosing what will be eaten for supper are all intertwined, connected, and interrelated according to what you will read in the coming pages.

The dichotomy between the secular and the spiritual that many hold onto in the West has in fact deeply affected our views on work, business, church and missions. In America, it is derived from the idea of separation of Church and State. Today, this concept has come to reflect the idea that religion and faith need to be quarantined from other aspects of secular life. It is often referred to in connection with Jesus' instruction to "render to Caesar what is Caesar's and to God what is God's." If that is our interpretation of this one Scripture passage, then we may miss the entire message of the biblical stories preceding this particular statement in which businessmen, kings, leaders, judges, crop owners and soldiers interconnected every aspect of their lives with the will of the Father. For the Chinese, life is not a list of boxes that remain separated, but, instead, it is a big ball of interconnected wires within which every aspect has purpose.

If this concept is not understood from the beginning, it may become an impediment to our understanding of what we can learn from the Chinese believers. For them, the dichotomy between the sacred and the secular simply does not exist.

BTJ is a part of a wider global movement within the Chinese underground house church, recognizing and responding to God's call to take the Gospel of Jesus Christ to the whole world, and (this is key) even to those parts that don't want it yet.

During the next 30 days, this devotional will allow you to peek into the minds and lives of the Chinese, to shed some of your cultural lenses and limited understanding of what it means to follow Christ, and to learn about the intimate lives of dedication and persecution of your brothers and sisters around the world.

Allow these next 30 days to take you on a journey of exploring a world that might be much different than your own and to transport you to places around the world where people are suffering and hurting every day but finding an unmarketable Joy of the Lord in that pain. May their burden become your burden. May their pain become your pain. May their vision become your vision.

As you read through these pages for only a few minutes each day, it is my hope that you can empathize with, and even relate to, believers who share the same faith as you, but whose day-to-day experiences more closely resemble those of the first century church.

During your daily devotions during the next 30 days, I pray that your life (those 20-30 minutes of it anyway) will be as miserable as that of the person you are reading about.

It might not be too late to pick up another book!

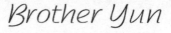

Brother Yun

Brother Yun is an exiled underground house church leader and evangelist. He was instrumental in the development of the underground House church networks that today have members numbering in the tens of millions.

He has been one of the most vocal international voices of the Chinese vision to take the gospel to every tribe and nation between China and Jerusalem. Brother Yun has spoken to more people in more countries about the Back to Jerusalem vision than any other person on earth.

He is often referred to as the Heavenly Man, as is explained in his bestselling autobiography called The Heavenly Man, in which he writes of both extreme persecution and miraculous deliverance similar to testimonies found in the Bible.

During his early days of ministry in Shaanxi Province, China, Brother Yun was arrested for preaching the gospel. Soon he found himself lying on his back with a police officer pinning him down by his neck.

When the police officers realized that they had apprehended a well-known preacher of Christianity, they tightly bound him with rope and made him stand up. Seeing a wooden cross on the wall, they mockingly took it down and tied it to Brother Yun's back.

They struck him and kicked him repeatedly until he was bloodied and bruised and then used the rope to pull him down the street with a police car. As they paraded Brother Yun up and down the streets, they announced over the loud speakers of the car that he had come from Henan Province to preach about Jesus and would be severely punished. Brother Yun was forced to walk around the city for the better part of the day before he was taken back to the police station. There they continued to beat him severely during extended interrogation sessions, and would very possibly have killed him had he not miraculously escaped from his cell.

Seeing Brother Yun publicly humiliated and punished that day actually had the opposite effect on the people of the city than what the authorities had expected to happen. Instead of bringing fear upon the population and keeping them away from the teachings of the Gospel message, the persecution of Yun caused the crowds to be moved with compassion and curiosity as they watched this man who was willing to be beaten and bloodied for his faith in Jesus Christ.

"Many people in the world today are working hard

to become leaders," Brother Yun said during a meeting in Texas in 2013. "Christians have been convinced that they need to study different methodologies of leadership and then implement them on the mission field in order to achieve better results for the kingdom of God.

"But I tell you that the last thing that this world needs today is another leadership training course for Christians. We have seen too much of it. I would like to see the leadership courses ripped up and thrown away. What we need is a course in servanthood. Our Leader taught us to be servants. Our leadership is through our servanthood. It is high time that the servants of Christ stop fighting with one another to be the top leader and start maneuvering themselves to be better servants.

"We are not merely called to be servants of Jesus Christ, but we are commanded to serve one another!"

THINK ABOUT IT

During a general Google search of Christian courses online, how many courses do you think can be found on leadership and how many on servanthood? Chinese Christians are not marching through the streets of China, demanding that their rights be recognized. They have not been leading political campaigns and human rights protests. Furthermore, Brother Yun has not sent one single letter to the government leaders of China, condemning them for any of the torture that he or his fellow believers have suffered at their hands. Instead, he prays for them.

Could this have anything to do with the largest revival in the world taking place in China today?

SCRIPTURE READING

Don't do anything for selfish purposes, but with humility think of others as better than yourselves. Instead of each person watching out for their own good, watch out for what is better for others. Adopt the attitude that was in Christ Jesus. Though He was in the form of God, He did not consider being equal with God something to exploit. But He emptied Himself by taking the form of a slave and by becoming like human beings. When He found Himself in the form of a human, He humbled Himself by becoming obedient to the point of death, even death on a cross.

Philippians 2:3-8

Pastor Zhang Rongliang

It is impossible understand the world's largest revival without looking into the history of the underground House church of China. It is equally impossible to tell the comprehensive story of the House church without a mention of Pastor Zhang Rongliang.

Pastor Zhang has been one of the most central (and sometimes most controversial) figures in all of China's underground house church. He is the founding pastor of one of the largest and most well-known underground House church networks called Fengcheng after the town of its origin.

Pastor Zhang has been arrested several times and has served several prison sentences during which he was beaten to a bloody pulp and left to rot in a prison cell. Here Pastor Zhang gives his view on suffering for Christ:

"The increasing number of Christians in China had an unforeseen side effect while I was in prison. More people were making visits to the prison to see me. It was a major turn of events. Sometimes it seemed that there was an endless stream of visitors making their way to the prison and requesting to see me.

"None of the government officials were happy about this. Having visitors come and spend time with me was very humbling as well as encouraging. I had renewed strength from the words that they shared with me and many of them expressed great admiration for my privilege of being a prisoner for the sake of the Lord.

"One of the visitors from Fengcheng County church asked me what I thought about the subject of suffering. I pondered that question for hours and my feelings about it will be hard to understand for those who have not experienced what I have been through.

"Christians are peculiar people and I consider myself to be a proud member of the Church. My take on suffering is one that I often pondered on. Suffering had been walking with me since my journey started with the Lord, but it was not the only experience I have had. My suffering has always been peppered with intense moments of joy and bliss.

"When I found myself alone with my thoughts, I decided to write down in my journal my understanding of the meaning of suffering:"

Suffering challenges so many people in the world. Without suffering how is it possible to taste the depths of the goodness of the Lord? After tasting of it, how can one be obsessed with worldly desires?

Oh Suffering, I used to flee from you. But today the Lord has commanded me to endure all that you have for me.

Oh Suffering, did the apostles not welcome you? Suffering invites the seekers to go along with him. He calls out to me and says, "Come and shake my hand."

Oh Suffering, let me embrace you. It tastes good that I was one with you in the Lord.

Oh Suffering, how many disciples have you fed? Without you, life has lost its struggle. I ask you to visit me. Let me taste only a bit of the sweetness that you give.

Oh Suffering, you make the moments with my Lord so much better. You are the oxygen of the saints. Without you, they would have stopped breathing. You are so close to me.

Oh Suffering, let us walk arm-in-arm together.

[Written from Xihua Prison]

THINK ABOUT IT

Have you ever in your life heard anyone ask suffering to come and embrace them? Many preachers and teachers in America and Europe emphasize that Jesus will give you the desires of your heart, but the Chinese believe that our flesh should be crucified daily as we pick up our cross and follow Christ. As we become more like Jesus, the desires of our hearts mimic His. What the heart once desired soon morphs into a strange brew of new desires that the world sees as just plain crazy.

Who are the ones more likely to go to the hard places to reach the lost, those who passionately seek after gifts of comfort, honor, and wealth or those who embrace suffering as a gift from God?

SCRIPTURE READING

My brothers and sisters, think of the various tests you encounter as occasions for joy. After all, you know that the testing of your faith produces endurance. Let this endurance complete its work so that you may be fully mature, complete, and lacking in nothing.

James 1:2-4

Day 3

Esther

On June 15, 2009 Ri Hyon Ok, a 33-year-old mother of three, was executed in Ryongchon city near the Chinese border for distributing Bibles in North Korea. Three children had their mother taken from them just because she handed out Bibles!

Not satisfied with murdering this poor mother, the authorities sent her entire family, children and all, to a prison camp. The most conservative estimates say there are more than 40,000 Christians in North Korean concentration camps but the number is thought to be as high as 90,000. According to the US government there are more than 6,000 Christians imprisoned in Prison Camp No. 15 alone.

According to numerous eyewitness accounts, Christians receive much harsher treatment than other inmates at these camps.

Christians are one of the most persecuted groups of people around the world and are being persecuted in places like China, India, Iran, and Saudi Arabia, but North Korea is unique in the world of Christian persecution. North Korea is continually ranked as the most oppressive country in the world for Christians and in many ways is in a league of its own.

In North Korea, Christians are not just killed, but are sent to death camps, run over by steamrollers, forced to watch the murders of their loved ones, forced to abort their children, and brutally executed in a myriad of ways.

Kim Il Sung himself said, "Anti-government behavior and enemies of the state must be annihilated to the third generation." This murderous principle is applied rigorously to those considered a threat to the government—especially Christians.

One defector told a US commission about his memories as a soldier in the North Korean army. He can remember when his unit was dispatched to clear the ground of obstacles so that a road between Pyongyang and Nampo could be widened.

In 1996, his unit began tearing down a vacant house in Yongkang County that was in the construction zone. When they began to tear down the foundation, they found a small notebook in the debris. Upon inspection, it turned out to contain a church roster with the names of a pastor, two assistant pastors, and other local Christians.

The contraband was immediately handed over to the authorities. The 25 people who were listed in the notebook were arrested and brought to the road construction site. Five of those detained were listed as leaders in the notebook and were bound and laid down on the ground. The other twenty were forced to stand on the side.

Announcements were quickly made in surrounding areas in order to assemble more observers to the punishment site. The five Christian leaders lay on the ground while a large steamroller was positioned in front of them. They were told to reject Jesus Christ and serve only Kim Il Sung and his son Kim Jong Il or they would die. None of the Christian leaders said a word.

They were given another chance to save their lives. These five leaders were told that they could continue living their lives and things would go back to the way they were if they would only deny the name of Jesus Christ.

They were given the same options that Nebuchadnezzar gave Shadrach, Meshach, and Abednego before the flaming furnace and that the Romans gave countless Christians as they faced roaring lions.

The fellow Christians in the crowd began to cry out, begging the leaders to do whatever necessary to save their lives. Their friends and family members could not bear to watch the horrid execution that was about to take place.

The steamroller started up. The ultimatum was offered again: Reject Jesus and live or refuse to deny Him and die. They remained silent. They had made their choice. It was clear that they would rather die than deny the wonderful name of Jesus Christ.

The steamroller began to roll towards the pastor,

the assistant pastors, and the elders and slowly drove over their bodies, crushing them to death. Onlookers said that they could hear the sound of the skulls popping as the steamroller ran over their heads. Some of the Christians who knew the pastor fainted when they saw the crushed bodies.

This took place in 1992, around the same time that Esther, a young mother from China, was called to North Korea.

Esther is one of the few people in the world to have been arrested in both North Korea and China and to live to tell about it.

Soon after going into North Korea, Esther was able to help the poor and to secretly share the gospel with them. Her humanitarian efforts caught the attention of many Communist Party leaders who insisted that she come and join them for an official government dinner a huge honor for anyone.

At first she respectfully refused the invitation, but the Party Secretary continued to insist on her attendance. He even sent an official government car to pick her up. This was a great honor, and it would have been politically disastrous for her to continue to refuse.

"Esther, you have done many great things for the Motherland," the Party Secretary said, as he kept heaping praises upon her.

After driving for some time they finally arrived at a bronze statue of Kim Il Sung, the founder of North Korea. The driver stopped and everyone got out of the car. It was customary for officials to pay their respects to large statues of the country's past and current leaders and to bow before them in worship.

Esther began to pray frantically in her spirit, knowing that this short moment could mean the end of her time in North Korea. If she refused to bow to the "Great Leader" in worship, she may be forced to leave the country or perhaps be put in jail. Locals could even be executed for refusing to bow before the Great Leader's statue.

As they walked together toward the statue, Esther was still at a loss as to how to handle the situation. Everyone lined up shoulder to shoulder beside each other and prepared to begin the ceremony.

"Dear Lord, what do you want me to do?" Esther prayed silently. Then suddenly a surge of boldness filled her heart and she began to pray differently.

"Kim Il Sung, you are not the King of Kings. You are not the Lord of Lords. You were a horrible, evil leader and I command you in the Name above all names to fall down and disappear!"

Everyone bowed in unison except Esther. She stood upright and stared directly at the bronze statue.

"Fall down in acknowledgement of the one and only King of Kings," she prayed in her spirit.

The statue did not fall physically, but it no longer held any power over Esther. After bowing several times, there were a few people who did notice that Esther did not bow.

"Teacher?" one of the Party members asked. They often called her teacher as a sign of respect in Korean culture.

"Why don't you bow when we come together and

pray before our Great Leader?"

"Please understand," Esther started slowly, "I don't know how to greet others by bowing down. After all, isn't it only a bronze statue? It isn't the Great Leader himself. He didn't make it; someone made it to remind them of him. The statue can't do anything to acknowledge that I have been here paying my respects. If I wanted to truly honor the Great Leader, wouldn't it be better to do something for him or his people directly? Which would be better for you, to follow the teachings of your leader and help those around you, or to come and bow to a statue that can't do anything for you, the people, or the Leader?"

The people around her pondered her words for a moment. From that day onward, they never again asked her to bow before the statue.

Many people reading this story might think that they would boldly tell the officials that Jesus Christ is Lord, not Kim Il Sung. However, Esther had a burden for the people of North Korea. She wanted to share the gospel with them, and she could not do that if she was kicked out of the country for making a brash statement to government officials.

Everywhere she looked in North Korea there were people hurting, afraid, and looking for a way out of their misery. They were like people waiting to be saved in the midst of a raging storm.

Esther began to secretly visit different homes in the dead of night to share the gospel with complete strangers.

She headed out after most people had gone to

bed. The lack of streetlights in North Korea made her feel unsafe at times, but the darkness also concealed her movement. Some friends had told her where to go, so the first couple of homes were expecting her. It was safer to meet in the privacy of a home at night when no one else was around to listen.

Esther continued to visit people's homes from that night on. She would sometimes spend all night preaching in one home. Not many people had lamps, so they would use fabric from blankets that Esther had brought from China, twist a strip of the cloth into a makeshift wick, and dip it in cooking oil to burn for light.

"Do not expect anything from me," she would say. "I am not capable of helping anyone and have no power to rescue you from your problems. I don't have all the answers, but I know the Answer—Jesus, the living God. He is not dead like your former leader Kim Il Sung."

The people in the room gasped at the notion that their Great Leader was dead. The North Korean government taught that Kim Il Sung was not dead but had become the eternal leader of the Korean people, so when a Korean died, they would be reunited with him. To Esther, that notion sounded more like living hell than like heaven.

"The God who lives can touch you where you need it the most. He can heal your broken heart, and all you have to do is ask him. Only the one true God can give you eternal life. Believe in Jesus with all your heart and only then can you be saved from eternal damnation. I have no material wealth, but if you look to the living God, He can meet your needs."

The people had never heard any teaching of this kind before. They were moved by Esther's boldness and passion. They were captivated by the fact that a woman was brave enough to defy the law of Kim Jong Il. She became known as the woman who did not bow to Kim Il Sung.

THINK ABOUT IT

Few people realize the tightrope that missionaries are constantly walking between effectiveness and counter-productive behavior. Christians that want a quick spotlight can easily travel to a closed country, challenge authority by boldly preaching the gospel, and get kicked out without ever seeing anyone saved. But hey—at least they have a cool story to put up on Facebook!

Esther prayed for wisdom. She didn't want to offend the authorities, but she also couldn't bow to Kim Il Sung. Her desire to stay with the people that did not know Jesus was so great that she, at various times in her life, went through some of the worst suffering that we can even imagine. She prayed for wisdom and God answered.

SCRIPTURE READING

Although I'm free from all people, I make myself a slave to all people, to recruit more of them. I act like a Jew to the Jews, so I can recruit Jews. I act like I'm under the Law to those under the Law, so I can recruit those who are under the Law (though I myself am not under the Law). I act like I'm outside the Law to those who are outside the Law, so I can recruit those outside the Law (though I'm not outside the law of God but rather under the law of Christ). I act weak to the weak, so I can recruit the weak. I have become all things to all people, so I could save some by all possible means. All the things I do are for the sake of the gospel, so I can be a partner with it.

I Corinthians 9:19-23

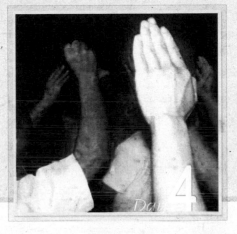

Pastor Shen Xiao Ming

One of the most well-known House churches in China is called China Gospel Fellowship (CGF). Of the five large underground House church networks, this is likely the most renowned.

As one of the early founders of the CGF network, Pastor Shen Xiaoming's personal account of growing up under Chairman Mao, witnessing massive revival in Henan Province, and seeing the formation of the China Gospel Fellowship is truly valuable. Pastor Shen writes:

"On December 10, 1957, I was born in a southern village of Henan Province. Those were times when Chinese government reports of agricultural abundance were empty and false. According to the Communist Party, each acre of land could yield many thousands of pounds of crops, even tens of thousands, but in reality the land yielded nothing and the people of China were starving. Everyone showed signs of malnutrition.

"Tens of thousands of people died in the Mao-made disaster. In the village where I lived, all the tree bark had been consumed. People ate it. It was all that they had to eat. Things were so bad that we even ate goose excrement.

"Things did not seem to improve much when I became a Christian evangelist. The only thing that changed was the added fear of being arrested.

"As evangelists, we constantly reminded each other that we must always be ready to go to jail. However, to keep this from happening too early in my ministry, I kept my hair short so that the police would not have anything to grab onto when I ran from them. I would also loosen all the buttons on my shirt before starting a meeting. I did this for the first ten years of ministry. Many of us evangelists would go many days without a shower, and our clothes became our blankets at night. We often slept in open fields or cowsheds, so many of us had gnats on our bodies and when we would get bored we would pick them off of each other.

"Once, in prison, I didn't have a Bible.

All I could do was to meditate on the verses I had memorized and to silently pray to God for strength to overcome in the midst of my suffering. I soon realized that God had answered my prayer for strength, as I never desired an early release from prison. When such thoughts surfaced, I immediately prayed for God to strengthen me and to give me resolve.

"At the end of those first years of evangelism we had established more than 200 host networks. Each time we had a meeting we spoke to gatherings of people in the hundreds. Everywhere we went, entire villages would swarm the meeting places. From those meetings, evangelists were sent out to preach the gospel in the surrounding cities and towns. Within two years we saw more than 30,000 people come to the Lord."

THINK ABOUT IT

One way that Pastor Shen prepared for his daily meetings was by wearing the type of clothes that ensured that he would have the highest probability of escaping from the authorities. What Western denomination would need to provide that type of clothing for their preachers and pastors?

Notice how Pastor Shen did not pray for early release from prison, but instead prayed for the strength to endure. God always brings purpose to our suffering, and He is in control of every situation that we encounter in our lives. While His will may be beyond our understanding and quite difficult for us to swallow, we can learn from Pastor Shen's example the importance of praying for God's will to be done above all else.

SCRIPTURE READING

But Saul grew stronger and stronger. He confused the Jews who lived in Damascus by proving that Jesus is the Christ. After this had gone on for some time, the Jews hatched a plot to kill Saul. However, he found out about their scheme. They were keeping watch at the city gates around the clock so they could assassinate him. But his disciples took him by night and lowered him in a basket through an opening in the city wall.

Acts 9:22-25

Day 5

Pastor Chen

Pastor Chen is the current representative for Tanghe underground House church network, one that today holds several million members.

"I became a believer in the winter of 1989, during a time when miracles were frequent in Tanghe. I was almost immediately enrolled into the underground Tanghe Bible School. This was not a legal, official Bible school, but it was all that we had. After completing the training course, I was sent to minister in Hebei Province for a year, Anhui Province for two or three years, and then to Hubei for six months.

"That is how we usually do it in China. Even before we attend any formal training we are expected to share with others. The need is too great to allow new believers time to get comfortable with the idea of being Christians. Once I became a believer, I was put to work right away,"

Pastor Chen said in an interview in Beijing in 2011.

Brother Yun spoke about the nature of this immersion technique utilized by the home churches in China during a meeting in Baton Rouge, Louisiana, in May of 2011. During his sermon he stated that the longer that Christians wait to be used, the less likely they are to ever be used. Brother Yun explained that in China, unlike in western cultures, new Christians are expected to immediately take what they know about Christ and share it with others. He went on to note that many people in the West feel that they must first receive formal training and a diploma that supposedly grants them legitimacy to preach, and only then might they go out and tell others about Christ.

The immersion technique is one of the most important practices contributing to the growth of Christianity in China today. When speaking about this technique, Brother Yun often points to Mary Magdalene and reminds his listeners that she didn't know much about where Jesus had gone or what He had been doing since his crucifixion, but immediately went and told others that Jesus had risen and that His tomb was empty.

The longer a believer waits to share his or her faith, the less likely they are to share it at all, even after much study. Pastor Chen did not have to wait long before he was thrown into the heat of battle. Because workers were in such short supply, he was often called upon to help carry and deliver Bibles from Guangzhou.

In 2002, Pastor Chen was sent to Beijing and was able to plant more than thirty churches that are now regularly attended by more than 2,800 believers. Those churches in Beijing are now sending evangelists to Gangsu, Xinjiang, and Qinghai Provinces to share the gospel with the Muslim minorities living there.

THINK ABOUT IT

You may be surprised to learn that (according to Faith Communities Today research) there appears to be a negative correlation between pastors' seminary education and congregation vitality. Pastors with master's degrees or doctorates from seminaries are less likely to be serving in flourishing congregations and more likely to be in congregations with conflict. According to the study, larger congregations are less likely to have pastors with seminary credentials.

Based on interviews with 601 Senior Pastors nationwide in America, representing a cross-section of Protestant churches, George Barna found that only one-half had a biblical worldview. The center for Cognitive Studies at Tufts University further found that many Christians graduate seminary as agnostics or even atheists.

Brother Yun continues to insist that prison was the best place for him to receive his Christian leadership training—in servanthood.

SCRIPTURE READING

Jesus came near and spoke to them, "I've received all authority in heaven and on earth. Therefore, go and make disciples of all nations, baptizing them in the name of the Father and of the Son and of the Holy Spirit, teaching them to obey everything that I've commanded you. Look, I myself will be with you every day until the end of this present age."

Matthew 28:18-20

Sister H

One story that had never been publicly told before was written about in BTJ's book "Crimson Cross." It is the story of one of the most effective training centers in all of China during the early 1990s. As the House church in China grew, so too did the need for competent leaders. However, many of the Chinese Christians didn't even own Bibles, let alone having received Bible training.

Congregating in unauthorized meetings was strictly forbidden in China in the early days, so a secluded place had to be found to train the future leaders in China. The location that the leaders agreed upon was in a cave.

More top leaders of today's underground House church were trained there than in any other single location in China.

Sister H had the vision for the cave and dug it out

literally with her own hands. Sister H's key role in transforming the underground House church movement has never really been mentioned before.

In the late 1980s, Brother Yun had very few people that he could rely on to hide him and his family from the authorities. The persecution from the government was intense and it was taxing on his whole family. Sister H prayed for Brother Yun on a regular basis while he was in prison and was deeply concerned for him and his family. Many nights she was unable to sleep because she was up praying for him and asking God to keep him safe.

Brother Yun's preaching was full of joy and without compromise, but his family had been paying a huge price for the work. His wife and children were constantly harassed and publicly humiliated for his "crime" of proselytizing in China.

In 1989 the revival began to spread uncontrollably from the rural farming communities to the more affluent cities where university students and even government officials were getting saved. As the multitude grew, so did the demand for shepherds to lead them.

The people were so hungry for the gospel that they would pack into small spaces to hear the preachers and wouldn't leave. The pastors would have to be carried in the air, over the crowd, in order to get out the door and onto the next meeting.

Sister H had a home in a place called Jingwa Town in Nanyang County. God led her to prepare a place in her home for Brother Yun to pray when he was released from prison. Beside her stove in the kitchen was a stack of firewood that she used for cooking and heating her home. She had the idea of removing the firewood and creating a small secret space big enough for one person to enter. The entrance could then be re-concealed with the firewood.

"So my husband and I dug out a small place in the side of the mountain and covered it with rocks so that it would look like the rest of the wall," Sister H recalled.

"Behind the area where the firewood was kept was a soft limestone area in the mountain that allowed for us to dig out this small space by hand. We dug out an area that was big enough for two people to squeeze into. That became a safe place for Brother Yun to pray in."

The prayer closet did not remain a prayer closet for long. Sister H, along with three other people, eventually dug out a cave large enough for a small Bible school. They dug it out all by hand.

"It would not have been safe to make it any larger," Sister H said. "The cave felt quite safe and secure, but if we would have been greedy and tried to make it even bigger, then we could have had the entire thing come down on us."

"If the police would have known what we were doing," she said, "They would have...(she put her fingers up to her head to signal a gun being pointed at her temple). During those days if the police would have known that I had a secret cave where I hosted meetings like this they would have executed me."

Several thousand believers were trained in that small, hand-dug cave.

THINK ABOUT IT

China's economy, politics, and military posturing are reshaping the world we live in. The United States, Europe, and the U.N. are currently rewriting their strategies because of China's growing influence around the globe. That same China is being uncontrollably shaped by its growing number of Christians and has seen more people come to Christ in the last twenty years than any other country in the world. The revival that China is currently experiencing is directly linked to a small cave in Henan Province that was dug out by the hands of one little lady who had a vision from God.

Sister H, in the hands of God, has changed the world that you live in.

SCRIPTURE READING

You are saved by God's grace because of your faith. This salvation is God's gift. It's not something you possessed. It's not something you did that you can be proud of. Instead, we are God's accomplishment, created in Christ Jesus to do good things. God planned for these good things to be the way that we live our lives.

Ephesians 2: 8-10

Pastor Chen

Truth Network is one of the House church networks more shrouded in mystery than any other network in China. Very little information is available about its history, founder, leadership, or activities. BTJ's book "Crimson Cross" may have been the first time that this network was ever written about.

If the Truth Network were an individual, she would be tagged as the strong silent type. Truth does not make much noise or garner much public attention, but without a doubt this network is making the largest impact for world missions today, if measured by the amount of money spent annually on missions or the number of missionaries sent out from China, and is arguably one of the largest underground House church networks in China today.

Pastor Chen is currently the pastor of Truth

Network. In 2003, he was one of the top six wanted criminals in all of eastern China. In February 2012, Pastor Chen came to Shanghai and told the amazing story of how Truth Network began.

"After the 1960s," says Chen, "It was not easy for any of the Christians left in China. They relied a lot on foreign missionaries. The foreigners read the Bible for them. They preached for them, led the churches, and led the prayers. When the foreigners left, the old Chinese Christians were not sure of anything. They didn't know how to pray and they didn't have a strong understanding of the Bible. They only knew that Jesus was God.

"I cannot really point to one single person who came and shared the gospel with us. During the days of Mao Zedong, my village area was one of the poorest in China. The villagers went mad. They were demon possessed. We didn't know it then, but there were entire villages that were possessed by demons."

The villages in and around Yinshang County had so many people who had lost their minds because they had no hope. There were no hospitals to go to for diagnoses and there was no money to pay for any treatment even if the diagnoses were clear. Pastor Chen was born in 1956 and was raised in Yinshang County during the darkest years of Chinese history. His family lived close to the bank of the Huai River and had experienced their share of hardships. The family had a history of cancer and deafness. Chen's grandfather went deaf at an early age and died of cancer. His father went completely deaf and died of cancer at the age of thirty-one.

Pastor Chen continues: "When I was younger I realized that I was going deaf. In 1979 I was almost completely deaf in both ears and was detecting signs of early cancer in my body. I was sick and too weak to move. I knew that my time on earth was not going to last much longer. One of my in-laws came and shared the gospel with me and it was at that time that I accepted Jesus as my Lord. On that day I was completely healed. No one could explain it. We didn't know how it worked. We only knew that it was the name of Jesus that had healed me.

"That is how the church grew in Yinshang in the early days. The biggest attraction was the casting out of demons. People were bringing to the Christians their demon-possessed family members who were out of control, and the demons would immediately leave when the family members received prayer.

"In Yinshang, ancestoral worship and tormenting from demons is a deeply-rooted cultural practice. Fengshui is based on this idea of creating good qi so that all forces flow naturally without stopping the flow of dragons or demons. The positioning of wind chimes and mirrors is very important in the Fengshui practiced in Anhui. Houses, rooms, and all other structures were built in ways deemed non-offensive to demons. The lives of the people were focused on appeasing the demons so that they would not torment the family.

"So many people were being set free from demons that there was no doubt about the power of the name of Jesus. We didn't know how to pray. We didn't have a Bible. We didn't know anything except what the old Christians told us regarding crying out in the name of Jesus.

"During the 1980s to 1990s there wasn't a farmer left in the field on Sunday. Everyone flocked to the name of Jesus. Our village went from a village with no believers to a village where everyone was a believer. Even today if you travel to Yingshan County you will find that almost everyone you meet is a believer in Jesus Christ."

THINK ABOUT IT

How many people fear doing anything for the sake of the gospel because they don't know enough about the Bible? One of the largest House church networks in China (estimated to contain more than 10 million believers) was started in a small village that didn't even have one single Bible. No one could quote the Scriptures, but they knew the name of Jesus had power—very real power.

To the critical thinking observer, this seems to be an open door to heresy and cults, but demons were cast out, the sick were healed and the deaf could hear. These were all very powerful demonstrations of the gospel of Jesus Christ flying in the face of the apparent biblical ignorance that was present in the Chinese village.

How does this line up with your understanding of how God works? How does this sum up the attendance record of seminars, conferences, church services, book purchases and online resources that most of us accumulate over the years? How many Bibles do you have at home (including those on your phone and computer)? Are you getting your money's worth? Better yet—is God getting His money's worth out of you?

SCRIPTURE READING

Heaven is declaring God's glory; the sky is proclaiming his handiwork. One day gushes the news to the next, and one night informs another what needs to be known. Of course, there's no speech, no words—their voices can't be heard—but their sound extends throughout the world; their words reach the ends of the earth.

God has made a tent in heaven for the sun. The sun is like a groom coming out of his honeymoon suite; like a warrior, it thrills at running its course. It rises in one end of the sky; its circuit is complete at the other. Nothing escapes its heat.

The Lord's Instruction is perfect, reviving one's very being. The Lord's laws are faithful, making naive people wise. The Lord's regulations are right, gladdening the heart. The Lord's commands are pure, giving light to the eyes.

Honoring the Lord is correct, lasting forever. The Lord's judgments are true. All of these are righteous! They are more desirable than gold—than tons of pure gold! They are sweeter than honey—even dripping off the honeycomb!

No doubt about it: your servant is enlightened by them; there is great reward in keeping them. But can anyone know what they've accidentally done wrong? Clear me of any unknown sin and save your servant from willful sins. Don't let them rule me. Then I'll be completely blameless; I'll be innocent of great wrongdoing.

Let the words of my mouth and the meditations of my heart be pleasing to you, Lord, my rock and my redeemer.

Psalm 19

Day 8

Pastor Zhang Rongliang

My Grandfather Sun opened up the Bible to Isaiah chapter 53 and began reading verses 2 through 6 to me. Instead of reading what it said, he replaced some of the words with my name to read like this:

"He had no beauty that Zhang Rongliang should desire Him. He is despised and rejected by Zhang Rongliang. A man of sorrows and acquainted with grief; and Zhang Rongliang hid as it were his face from Him. He was despised and Zhang Rongliang esteemed Him not. Surely He has borne Zhang Rongliang's griefs and carried his sorrows, yet Zhang Rongliang did esteem Him stricken, smitten of God and afflicted. But He was wounded for Zhang Rongliang's transgressions, He was bruised for Zhang Rongliang's iniquities; the chastisement of Zhang Rongliang's peace was upon Him and with His stripes Zhang Rongliang was healed. Zhang Rongliang is like a sheep who has gone astray, Zhang Rongliang has turned everyone to his own way; and the Lord has laid on Him the iniquity of Zhang Rongliang."

After hearing that, I couldn't help but weep over the guilt of my sin and the high price that the Lord had paid to take it from me. From that day on, I decided to follow after Christ. The way Grandfather Sun read that passage has stayed with me until this day and I will never forget it.

My older sister was also a Christian and went to church. One time she took me to church with her. It all seemed very mysterious to me since our culture didn't have much exposure to Christianity.

The only thing that I really remember is everyone praying together. My sister leaned over and told me, "Zhang, you are supposed to close your eyes when we pray." I didn't know why. I thought you were supposed to close your eyes because something very mysterious and scary was about to happen and you weren't supposed to watch it. I didn't know that there was a time to close your eyes at the beginning of prayer and open your eyes at the end of prayer, so I kept my eyes closed even after the prayer was over.

When I heard people say, "Amen," I didn't know what they meant. I just kept my eyes closed. Even when everyone was done praying and it was time to go home, I kept my eyes closed. I held on to my sister's hand and she led me out of the church without looking at me. When we left the church and were walking home, she realized that I still had my eyes closed.

"What are you doing? Why are your eyes closed,"

she asked.

"You told me to close my eyes!"

"Yes, but that is during prayer. We are not praying anymore. You can open them now."

It occurred to me that maybe the scary and mysterious things only happened when people were praying at church. In those days I wasn't too familiar with the activities of the church and associated some of them with Chinese superstition.

Not long after, Grandfather Sun was publicly humiliated and tortured. He was brought out by local officials and forced to walk down our hometown street with a board hanging around his neck. Written on it in huge letters was the phrase, "Follower of Jesus."

He was marked as an anti- revolutionary and humiliated by the Communist Party.

A long hat resembling a western dunce cap was made out of newspaper and put on his head. He looked like a helpless lamb among wolves.

Before he died, he looked at me and said, "My boy. I believe the Lord will greatly use you for His purpose. I am going home now. Remember this with all your might: continue to preach the Good News of Jesus Christ whether the time is right or not."

Those words stay with me even now. They linger in my memory and have been stamped on my mind as the true mark of sacrifice: "....whether the time is right or not."

THINK ABOUT IT

Pastor Zhang Rongliang's grandfather could have easily felt like a complete failure and died feeling like he had never had the chance to make a difference in this world. He was poor. He never traveled outside a one-hundred mile radius. He wasn't highly educated. He was never elected to office. He wasn't born to a famous family. He never led an army. He never wrote a book. He never did any of the things that we associate with greatness, yet his words changed the heart of Zhang Rongliang.

Read the underlined lines above again. Those statements are true for Zhang Rongliang's grandfather, but they are also true about Jesus.

For our scripture reading today, let's take the advice of an old simple Chinese grandfather who was marched through the streets of Henan Province for the sake of Christ and insert our own names in the blanks.

SCRIPTURE READING

He had no beauty that _____ should desire Him. He is despised and rejected by _____. A man of sorrows and acquainted with grief; and _____ hid as it were his face from Him. He was despised and _____ esteemed Him not. Surely He has borne_____ griefs and carried his sorrows, yet _____ did esteem Him stricken, smitten of God and afflicted. But He was wounded for _____ transgressions, He was bruised for _____ iniquities; the chastisement of _____ peace was upon Him and with His stripes _____was healed. _____ is like a sheep who has gone astray, _____ has turned everyone to his own way; and the Lord has laid on Him the iniquity of _____.

Isaiah 53:2-6

A Chinese Believer

BTJ often receives letters of appreciation for the Bibles we distribute every year. Bibles are still the number one need of the church in China today.

After years of seeing a dramatic increase in the number of Christians inside China, it has become clear that the number of Bibles and Christian teaching materials available there is not even a fraction of what is needed.

There are conservative estimates of 10 to 12 million new believers in China per year with an already 120 to 150 million believers currently in the country. Amity Press, located in Nanjing, China, is often touted as the largest Bible producer in the world. In 2008, the Amity Press website claimed that they had printed just over 10 million Bibles that year and celebrated printing 50 million Bibles since they had first started printing

Bibles in China. These Bibles, however, are not printed just for China. In fact, the majority of them are printed in other languages and sent to other countries, leaving a massive shortage of one of the most valued treasures for any believer.

Here is a letter from one believer in China who just received a Bible:

I received my own Bible by God's Grace! Praise the Lord!

Thank you for distributing the Bibles to our church. Because of your gift, I am able to preach the gospel to others. It is your love and donation and I receive it with a glad heart.

Soon after I received the Bible that you gave, I became a preacher. Since I received the Bible from you, I have established two churches and have led a total of 232 people to Christ. In the two churches that I have started, less than half of the congregations own a Bible.

To compensate for many of the listeners not owning a Bible, sometimes I will teach Bible verses and those in the church will listen and write down the verses in their own notebooks. That way they can read God's Word when they go home.

I am very thankful that I have a Bible now. My mother did not know how to read, but after

I gave her a Bible, miraculously she was able to read it. This is only by God's grace!

I really feel that there are too few people coming to the Lord every day, but I will continue to preach the gospel. We pray for you daily. May you be a great blessing for the people in this world.

God bless you and remember you!
Thank you!

THINK ABOUT IT

Chinese authorities continue to claim that smuggling Bibles to China is a waste of resources. Many ministries have echoed that sentiment. Even with the 6 million Bibles that the government claimed to have printed in 2007, the majority were for export only. The church is growing by 30,000 believers per day, or 10 to 12 million believers per year. The entire population of China is widely known to contain more than 1.4 billion people. So, in essence, are we to believe that 6 million Bibles (the majority for export) are enough for 1.4 billion people, with a growing Christian population of more than 30,000 believers per day?

To make this more clear, following this line of logic, the Norwegian capital city of Oslo would only be allowed to have 2,610 Bibles per year for the entire city (this includes only New Testament versions). Less than

1,000 people per year would be allowed to have a new complete Bible containing both Old and New Testaments if these rules were enforced on the Norwegian people.

New York would only be allowed to have 85,000 Bibles per year so that less than 40,000 people per year would be allowed to have both Old and New Testaments.

The town of Montpelier, Indiana would only be allowed to have eight Bibles for the entire town and that is INCLUDING the New Testament prints. That is not even one Bible for every two churches in the whole town! How many residents would be picking up their rifles in Montpelier, Indiana today if the Chinese laws of Bible distribution were enforced?

SCRIPTURE READING

Because God's word is living, active, and sharper than any two-edged sword. It penetrates to the point that it separates the soul from the spirit and the joints from the marrow. It's able to judge the heart's thoughts and intentions. No creature is hidden from it, but rather everything is naked and exposed to the eyes of the one to whom we have to give an answer.

Hebrews 4:12-13

Missionary Jason

The countries between China and Jerusalem are known in the missions world as the 10/40 Window. Two-thirds of the world's population lives in this window and nine out of every ten people who have never heard the gospel of Jesus Christ also live in this area.

Sadly, even though the majority of the people in the world and virtually all unevangelised people groups live in the 10/40 Window, less than one penny for every $100 USD given to missions is used here.

According a 2007 study by Baxter, 91% of all Christian outreach/evangelism does not target non-believers, but benefits other Christians. Of foreign mission funding, 87% goes for work among those that are already Christian, 12% for work among already evangelized but non-Christian, and 1% for non-evangelized and unreached people.

The opposite is true for Jason who comes from Henan, China. His home church has very few resources, but it uses the majority of them to support Jason and his family as they serve in South Sudan. Jason has been living in South Sudan since it first separated from the North.

In January 2013, he and his family were still living there even though a new civil war threatened their safety. Jason's family, along with another missionary team, are the first BTJ missionaries from China sent to live and serve in South Sudan. Here is one of his many testimonies from the last year:

"There is a well-known lady living in our area who is known to be demon possessed. Witchcraft and demon possession are common here among the tribes in South Sudan. She did not want to be controlled by evil spirits any longer and begged for someone to help her escape their torment.

"She asked one of the local Sudanese pastors for help, but he was not willing to help her. In December 2013, my coworker and I were invited to attend a local meeting with a body of new believers. They asked us to pray for the sick.

"As we began to pray, the demon possessed woman came forward and received prayer. It was an animated event. Suddenly she began to shout, 'I am free! The demon has left me! I am free!'

"Immediately she gave glory to Jesus for what He had done in her life. She shouted that she was free and she has remained healed from that moment on.

"I was encouraged and strengthened by her testimony. I am used to reading in the Bible about extraordinary miracles through Paul and the other apostles, and I believe their accounts of how the sick were healed and evil spirits were forced to flee, but have never thought that I would be witness to similar miracles in a place like South Sudan.

"Only God can truly understand how weak and ignorant I am. I can only bow down at His feet and trust in His Word. He makes me taste the joy and satisfaction of His presence. Our God is a healing God, and I believe that when we depend on him and lift his name on high, He will become our strength and help us to do His work. So we should go out with this simple faith, trusting in His power and not in our own and help and love those people who don't know God yet."

THINK ABOUT IT

Two out of three people in the world live in the 10/40 Window and only a fraction of the Christian body is making an effort to carry out the command that Jesus gave in Matthew 28:18-19. A believer without a high school diploma, raised in the poorest region of Communist China, has packed his bags to take the gospel message to the people in South Sudan. In the meantime, what are we doing with all that God has blessed us with?

SCRIPTURE READING

Jesus traveled among all the cities and villages, teaching in their synagogues, announcing the good news of the kingdom, and healing every disease and every sickness. Now when Jesus saw the crowds, he had compassion for them because they were troubled and helpless, like sheep without a shepherd. Then he said to his disciples, "The size of the harvest is bigger than you can imagine, but there are few workers. Therefore, plead with the Lord of the harvest to send out workers for his harvest.

Matthew 9:35-38

Brother "Q"

When I was 25 years old, I was called into full-time service to be God's servant. I had watched the amazing work of other evangelists in my hometown. I hoped to know Jesus more and I really wanted to serve Jesus like those evangelists did.

Shortly after jumping into full-time ministry, I began to serve by working in a fellowship that was a secret gathering in a local factory. I began to minister full-time in 2008 and that was a special time in China because the Olympics were coming to Beijing. Every thing was tense. Many Christian groups were targeted by the government during that period, especially small religious groups. Anyone suspected of being involved in religious activities was arrested. The government took a hard stance against all religious activities.

One day I was in the factory with twenty other

members of our church group. We had gathered for a worship service. The police came busting through the doors unexpectedly and arrested us all. I was sentenced to three years in a Chinese maximum-security prison and was placed in a cell with common criminals. It was as if I had committed murder or rape. I prayed that God would show me favor and deliver me, but deliverance never came.

Day after day I sat in my cell. I ate the same food and received the same punishment as all of the other inmates. I was not allowed to have a Bible with me, but was able to smuggle one in without the guards knowing. God's Word encouraged me every day. I read how Paul and Peter endured through severe circumstances. I also read how they too were in prison for the gospel. I felt like I was reading the Bible for the first time because I was reading it with the eyes of experience. I especially took notice of how they acted and what they spoke when they were in prison.

It was not long before I realized that being in prison was the single best thing that could have ever happened to me. I was a relatively new Christian and had many misconceptions about the Word of God, but I grew immensely during that period because I was confined with nothing else to do but to read the Bible.

I had to learn patience more than anything else. Being in prison taught me to wait upon the Lord and for His timing. I understood how to submit my will to His. I was a new Christian and had so very much to learn.

Thank God that He sent me to prison! He really encouraged me through the stories of Moses and David.

Not long after I arrived in prison, God sent an older believer who came alongside me and began to disciple me. He encouraged me to not give up. We became close friends and I learned that he was a pastor and a leader in a House church.

He was a big encouragement to me and has been an excellent mentor. Since my release in 2011, I have been serving in a local church. Today I feel equipped to preach about the dangers of living life with our own agenda, even if that agenda is for God.

THINK ABOUT IT

How often do we try to program God and stuff Him in a box? We print His allowed time on a bulletin and assign Him an hour and a minute when to show up and when to leave our church services. How often do we tell God to wait, go, stop, or come according to our own timetables?

Brother "Q" believed that God wanted him to be in prison. How does that line up with your ideas about God? Does your concept of God allow the schedules of man to rule God or does God rule over the schedules of man? As rhetorical as that question sounds, what evidence do you have of your beliefs?

Do we emulate God's love? God's love is multidimensional. The Chinese might be able to show us another side to God's love if we observe and are taught by them. To the Chinese believer, love is not just a feeling that is connected to romance and infatuation. It is patient, longsuffering, and carries the connotations of duty and service. Love does not necessarily require the immediate self-gratification of a warm embrace, but instead its manifestation might be better displayed in self-denial for the benefit of the one that is loved.

SCRIPTURE READING

It isn't happy with injustice, but it is happy with the truth. Love puts up with all things, trusts in all things, hopes for all things, endures all things.

Love never fails. As for prophecies, they will be brought to an end. As for tongues, they will stop. As for knowledge, it will be brought to an end. We know in part and we prophesy in part; but when the perfect comes, what is partial will be brought to an end. When I was a child, I used to speak like a child, reason like a child, think like a child. But now that I have become a man, I've put an end to childish things. Now we see a reflection in a mirror; then we will see face-to-face. Now I know partially, but then I will know completely in the same way that I have been completely known. Now faith, hope, and love remain—these three things—and the greatest of these is love.

I Corinthians 13:6-13

Day 12

Brother Yun

After I had started preaching on the streets of China, many people started to come to the Lord. These new believers, I don't even know who they were, became Jesus freaks. There was an explosion, but it wasn't because I was preaching to them. The new believers were going to their neighbors and family members and preaching the Good News to them. There was a ripple effect and the officials soon realized that multitudes of people were coming to Christ.

This seemed absurd to the officials because they couldn't understand how people could become Christian so quickly unless specific individuals were sharing with them and, after all, sharing the gospel was against the law.

When they looked to see who was behind all of these people hearing about Jesus, of course they found me and quickly identified me as the instigator of all their troubles. New believers were being arrested everywhere and many of them were telling the same story: Brother Yun shared this message of Jesus with me.

Overnight I became a counter-revolutionary. The government officials saw me as a national security threat. The first day that I was recognized as a "proper" pastor in China was when my posters began to pop up all over the city streets, marking me as a wanted criminal.

After I had been on the run for more than ten years, I was becoming extremely tired. The persecution kept me moving all the time. I could never stay in the same place for long. That was good for the spreading of the gospel and it was good to keep me from being arrested, but it was not good for my body. I didn't know how to rest and I was tired to the bone. Every part of me was completely exhausted and I just needed a break from everything.

Then the Lord spoke to me and said, "My child, I can see that you are tired. I have prepared a place of rest for you."

I was so excited when I heard those words from the Lord. I had never been on a vacation before and could only imagine what kind of glorious resort He was preparing for me to find refuge in so that I could rest. I dreamed about the day that I would find rest for my soul and body.

Running from the authorities and watching over your shoulder all the time is not the way anyone wants to live life. I was ready for the Lord to give me my well-deserved rest.

Before the Lord sent me on this vacation, He told me that I needed to first hold a discipleship-training meeting to train up my replacements for the time when I would be away.

Of course I didn't know what discipleship training meant or looked like. I had never heard of anything like it before in China. I really felt that I was not prepared in any way to train up disciples, but I did what the Lord commanded me to do.

I called together about 100 young and passionate believers who were hungry for the Lord and willing to give their lives for the calling. Once they were together I simply assigned each of them a book of the Bible to memorize in the New Testament.

I then explained to them that they were each a heavenly person. They have been called to a heavenly kingdom, their riches are not of this world, and this would forever be their new identity. They were no longer citizens of China, but now they were citizens of the Kingdom of God.

Only a couple of weeks after I left them, I was arrested. My vacation home was a Chinese prison and the Lord gave me the rest that I had so desperately needed.

What Brother Yun has experienced and what he has learned from his many difficult experiences has made him a unique witness around the world. Christians living in the West might have a problem with some of his theology, but believers who currently live in persecuted countries around the world find hope in Brother Yun's story. They are not only excited about what God has done in Yun's life, but about what He will do in their own countries as well.

These persecuted Christians are people like Iranian Pastor Saeed Abedini who read Brother Yun's testimony and traveled to Germany the first chance he had just to meet with him. Pastor Saeed has now been detained in an Iranian prison since the summer of 2012 and feels a unique connection to Brother Yun because of his experiences in Chinese prison.

THINK ABOUT IT

How could a prison cell in China possibly be called a place of rest? Did or would God really arrange such a thing for his beloved servant? Is the joy of believers dependent on their circumstances or, in contrast to current popular thought, is our faith in Jesus only fully manifested in the joy that we feel when we know that our situation is desperate? If our situation is never desperate, then how can one ever say that the "joy of the Lord" is one's strength?

Even the lazy and evil can experience joy when circumstances absolutely demand it, but it takes quite a different creature to bask in joy's warmth when the tempest shows no mercy and begs the question, "Where is your God?"

Satan will continually try to dilute our hope with perverted definitions of reality and tear us away from our Creator. One of the main enemies of joy is the idea that you have more control over the future than you do. The Chinese underground pastors often teach that joy is more easily obtainable when we are more dependent upon God and trust the future (and the present) to Him. Control is the antithesis of joy for Chinese believers.

The things that Brother Yun has learned behind the bars of prisons both in China and Burma have shaped the way that he reads the Bible today and the sermons that he shares around the world. Oftentimes persecuted Christians find comfort and solace in the things that others would find tragic and unbearable.

Brother Yun went to prison and he found rest, just as the Lord promised.

SCRIPTURE READING

My brothers and sisters, think of the various tests you encounter as occasions for joy. After all, you know that the testing of your faith produces endurance. Let this endurance complete its work so that you may be fully mature, complete, and lacking in nothing.

James 1:2-4

Pastor Zhang Rongliang

In 1963, after my father died, my mother remarried and we moved to another town called Guaihe to live with my new stepfather. It was a change for all of us. My mother's new husband did not have a job, so our financial situation didn't change much, but living in Guaihe did bring about other opportunities which had not been available to us before.

There were people throughout the village of Guaihe who kept sheep. The sheep were free-roaming and the locals needed someone to look after them. Guaihe was surrounded by mountains and we lived at the top of a mountain. It was the perfect place to look after sheep. Soon after we arrived there, people of the town chose me as one of the people to tend the sheep. The owners of the sheep didn't have enough money to pay to me, so they paid me by giving me sheep. Because we lived so high up on the mountain, we never really had anyone try to steal the sheep. Although human thieves were never a problem, a different kind of thief was. I always had to be on the lookout for wolves.

I got to know the sheep well because I lived with them and even slept together with them. I often led them to our home and kept them in our house in a space under the floor. Our home was elevated enough off the ground that livestock could live under our floor.

I gave each of the sheep a name and became quite close to them. I learned their personalities and saw that they were all unique and different. When I first started looking after the sheep I felt that they were all the same, but after spending time with them and getting to know them I realized that they were just as diverse as people are. Certain sheep were afraid and timid and others were brave and forceful. A few of them were curious and liked to explore far away from the herd while others were more cautious and never left the group.

There were even conflicts among the sheep that I would have to settle. This was my first course in conflict management that would later come in handy as a pastor. I had to become knowledgeable about the different kinds of grass and know what the sheep liked and didn't like.

I developed an emotional connection with the sheep and treated them when they were sick. I protected them from wolf attacks and helped keep them together so that they would not get lost. I also observed their fear and empathized with them when it was time to take them to slaughter. They really became like a second family to me.

The time that I spent shepherding sheep during those years would prove to be invaluable to me when I later served as a pastor in China's underground House church.

THINK ABOUT IT

Shepherding sheep seems to only be an occupation reserved for characters in the Bible, but when we learn more about Pastor Zhang Rongliang, we find that he too was a shepherd boy. Pastor Zhang is quite possibly the most well known pastor among the House church leaders today and is in charge of a church of several million believers.

According to him, the time that he spent with sheep was invaluable training before he became a pastor.

In Chinese culture, arranged marriage is still a continuing practice. Pastor Zhang and his wife were arranged to be married by a matchmaker in their village. Being a matchmaker is often the role of a village elder who is respected by others and understands the dynamics of the entire village and their families.

In the underground House church, network leaders often act as matchmakers and arrange marriages among their congregants. Some in western cultures might frown upon this, but these arranged marriages are closer to the culture of the Bible than today's western concept and the percentage of divorce is drastically lower among them than in any western society.

Pastor Zhang arranged the marriage of a young leader named Joshua and his wife who serve as leaders today in a network called "No Name Network" or simply "The Five Brothers." Joshua learned much from Pastor Zhang during his time of tutelage under him. He understands this idea of learning from animals like sheep and feels that it is essential.

Joshua runs a Bible training school for future missionaries, pastors, and evangelists. At the training school the students tend to a herd of goats every day. They not only feed them and look after them, but a shepherd is assigned to the goats on a rotating basis and takes them out to the mountains to free graze on the grass that grows there. The goats are not kept in a barn that is far removed from the students. The pastors-to-be live together in the same room, under the same roof as the goats. How is that for your idea of a Bible school?

SCRIPTURE READING

Shout triumphantly to the Lord, all the earth! Serve the Lord with celebration! Come before him with shouts of joy! Know that the Lord is God—he made us; we belong to him. We are his people, the sheep of his own pasture. Enter his gates with thanks; enter his courtyards with praise! Thank him! Bless his name! Because the Lord is good, his loyal love lasts forever; his faithfulness lasts generation after generation.

Psalm 100

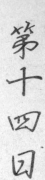

Day 14

Brother "Z"

Brother "Z" is a Back to Jerusalem missionary whom God called to minister in the Muslim world. A few years ago, Brother "Z", his wife, and his small daughter moved to Egypt to preach the gospel of Jesus Christ.

Brother "Z" didn't know much of the language, didn't understand the culture, and was not educated enough to obtain a well-paying job. He knew that God had called him to go, so he and his family went, putting their faith in the Lord.

"We found in Egypt that there were not many believers. After we learned a little about the culture, politics, and laws of Egypt we felt that it was wisest to be low-profile Chinese immigrants so that we could build relationships with the locals. Most Egyptians did not immediately assume that we were Christians, because we were Chinese. This helped us build quick relationships with the local people and share with them the gospel message. We had small meetings in our home so that it would be safer for those who converted.

"In Egypt, if the local people brought a complaint against us, it would be very easy for us to be kicked out. Our strategy was to pursue friendships with the Muslims whom God brought to us, and trust that He would give us opportunities to minister in that way.

"During the Revolution in Egypt, we were able to build up our relationships with the local Egyptians who lived in our building. Even though there was danger and uncertainty everywhere, we wanted to bring the peace of Jesus into the lives of others.

"We invited families over to our home and showed them how we pray before meals and demonstrated to them the love of Jesus. They were amazed at the level of freedom we had when we prayed to God before eating. We didn't have to stand, kneel, or quote endless memorized phrases in a synchronized manner. We speak to a living God who responds to the heart over ceremony.

"One family in our building became very sick, so the family came and asked us to go and pray for them. We immediately went up the stairs to their apartment and prayed for the sick boy. His sickness went away and he was healed.

"Because of our time in Egypt, we learned many things about Muslims. Many Muslims don't understand the Koran and aren't even familiar with what their prayers mean. They only repeat what they have been forced to learn.

"By sharing Jesus with the people in Egypt, we were able to see prisoners of Islam set free."

THINK ABOUT IT

For generations the Chinese have been referred to as Buddhists, Confucianists, Taoists, animists, and atheists by the rest of the world. Americans or Europeans are identified as Christians right away when they travel to a Muslim country, even if they are not.

Chinese have many generations of stereotyping in their favor that allows them to build relationships that might not be available to other missionaries. This rare opportunity that the Chinese have can easily allow them to move beyond the automatic defensive measures that a cultural Muslim might take towards Christianity. The Back to Jerusalem vision that God has given to the Chinese presents some of the most unique opportunities for gospel presentation that have been seen in generations.

SCRIPTURE READING

But God chose what the world considers foolish to shame the wise. God chose what the world considers weak to shame the strong. And God chose what the world considers low-class and low-life—what is considered to be nothing—to reduce what is considered to be something to nothing. So no human being can brag in God's presence. It is because of God that you are in Christ Jesus. He became wisdom from God for us. This means that he made us righteous and holy, and he delivered us. This is consistent with what was written: The one who brags should brag in the Lord!

I Corinthians 1:27-31

Day 15

Pastor Mary

The month of May 2008 proved to be a devastating time for China as the world watched the provinces of Gansu and Sichuan be violently shaken to their very foundations. More than 70,000 people lost their lives and more than 5 million people found themselves homeless without shelter or necessities for survival.

With the enormity of the disaster, China's leaders called on her people to help and the first ones to respond were the Christians from China's loathed underground House church. Back to Jerusalem quickly organized a collective effort to provide essential items to those who had lost everything.

Because so many of our Chinese partners worked in factories, they were well prepared for the production of necessary items. The Chinese Back to Jerusalem missionaries provided the necessary supplies at a faster rate and at a cheaper price than international aid organizations.

Basing their cost effectiveness on one report from Finland's Red Cross, the tents of equal quality that were provided by the Chinese missionaries cost less than one-sixth of the price that the Red Cross reportedly spent.

International organizations were using their aid money to purchase products that were originally made in China and were then packaged, shipped to the country of purchase, repackaged, and finally shipped back to China for distribution. In contrast, Chinese believers were able to produce their supplies at the source location and to bypass the unnecessary overhead in order to reach more people while requiring fewer resources

In the weeks following the earthquake, Chinese Christians from the underground House church were able to provide several tons of aid and supplies, as well as much needed grief counseling to victims of the quake. Back to Jerusalem missionaries started grocery stores, libraries, and restaurants in the disaster areas and were among the first to get business up and going again and to provide much-needed jobs to the locals. Libraries were set up in tent cities and freely distributed teaching materials, Bibles, and curriculums for children. As a result, many people gave their hearts to Christ. In one instance, an entire village became Christian.

Missionaries who had been working in the area prior to the earthquake had felt that it was virtually impossible to lead people to the Lord in the minority areas of Wenchuan and Beichuan, but after the earthquake hundreds, if not thousands, of people came to the Lord and gave their lives to Jesus Christ in these areas.

Churches were planted at a rapid rate throughout the earthquake disaster area among minority groups living in the foothills of Sichuan Province. Because of this, many pastors, evangelists, and aspiring missionaries relocated to Sichuan and Gansu Province.

Mary is such a worker who has been serving in Sichuan. She is a pastor who has been living and working in the earthquake area for several years. Some people might have a problem with the thought of a woman pastor, but Mary serves in an area where more than 80% of the believers and workers are women. She is a leader serving in a difficult and hostile area and this is her testimony:

"I belong to the (underground) House church. The meaning of the House church is that our meetings take place in homes of regular people. Before the earthquake there were not many Christians and not many people came to the home meetings. After the earthquake there were missionaries who came from all over China to share the gospel and to plant churches. The locals were very receptive and many churches were planted. There were many new groups of believers that were born out of the earthquake.

"Before 2008, our major challenge was getting people to listen to the Good News, but now our major challenge is persecution from the government. We have been attacked from different fronts. Last year there were many people in our church who were arrested. We had a guest pastor from Taiwan who came to preach at our church and during that time the police raided the home and all of the church members were detained.

"I was able to escape. The police know me very well and they soon came to my house to find me. They have come there many times in the past looking for me. One time they didn't find me at home so they beat my husband in order to persuade me to leave the church. However, we have found that even in the midst of persecution the church continues to grow. The members of our House church meet on Mondays instead of Sundays now in order to avoid detection by the police."

THINK ABOUT IT

Why do natural disasters happen in the world today? If there is a God, is He strong enough to stop them but chooses not to, thus making Him cruel, or would He like to stop them but can't, thus making him weak?

Which one is it? The world wants to know. Is God cruel or is He weak? Does He exist at all?

The Chinese rarely have this dilemma, because the question comes from a Judeo-Christian understanding of the world. The Chinese currently live in a society recovering from Mao Zedong's atheistic version of the world and have less of the residual Judeo-Christian beliefs of right and wrong and justice that exist in the West.

Pastor Mary accepts the fact that we live in a world that has been tainted and polluted by sin. The earth that God created was perfect in every way. There was no death and there were no diseases, but the sin of man set the world on a course where ALL THINGS go from order to chaos. Nevertheless, the Chinese also understand the biblical reality that God is still sovereign over all that is happening and will use ALL THINGS, even a devastating earthquake, to do good for His people. God is neither evil nor weak.

Pastor Mary knows that the Sichuan earthquake was not inflicted upon us by God, but is simply the result of living in a fallen world. Pastor Mary doesn't blame God every time the police break in through her door and attack her friends and family. She knows that it is the sin of man. Simply put, sin is choosing anything that is not of God.

God gave man free choice and with free choice we have the choice to choose God or that which is not of God. God is life, joy and love, but sin is just the opposite, bringing pain, hurt, injustice, darkness, and death.

In the midst of disaster, Pastor Mary teaches that when Jesus returns the lion will lay down with the lamb. He will build a new heaven and a new earth and all these hardships will pass away.

The Chinese underground House church believers have found that the pains of this world are overwhelming for those without the hope of Jesus Christ.

SCRIPTURE READING

The Son is the image of the invisible God, the one who is first over all creation, because all things were created by him: both in the heavens and on the earth, the things that are visible and the things that are invisible. Whether they are thrones or powers, or rulers or authorities, all things were created through him and for him. He existed before all things, and all things are held together in him. He is the head of the body, the church, who is the beginning, the one who is firstborn from among the dead so that he might occupy the first place in everything. Because all the fullness of God was pleased to live in him, and he reconciled all things to himself through him—whether things on earth or in the heavens. He brought peace through the blood of his cross.

Colossians 15-20

Day 16

Missionary Silas

Since the beginning of the Back to Jerusalem vision in the early 1900s, Chinese believers have been focused on taking the gospel into the Himalayan mountain regions.

To see that vision become reality, the underground home churches in China have been sending evangelists into Tibet, a place traditionally known to be one of the most challenging places to work in all of China.

The Tibetan Buddhists have been aggressively opposed to any other religion than Buddhism being preached in their country. Anyone with preconceived ideas of peaceful Buddhist followers meditating in fields full of flowers would be shocked to learn about the violent history of Buddhist attacks on Christian missionaries.

In the early 2000s Back to Jerusalem worked to

build a training center for Chinese missionaries in Tibet. The training center is not just a building taking up space in the middle of Tibet. It is a business that allows the Chinese believers to gain a skill while studying the Bible. The skills that they learn allow them to continue on the Silk Road and be productive in other countries.

Simon was one of the missionaries who traveled to Tibet to serve and work at the training center. He preached the gospel during the Tibetan riots in 2008. The skills that he learned while working at the Back to Jerusalem training center in Tibet have proven to be priceless.

Missiology is theology in action. In other words, it is where the rubber meets the road. It is important for missionaries to capitalize on the geographical location of training centers like the one in Tibet and to utilize them to fulfill the mandate given by Jesus Christ.

The training center in Tibet is not an elite institution encouraging the academic regurgitation of information that cannot be practically implemented on the field or effectively replicated. It provides training that is raw and relevant because it is on-the-job training.

"Where we live is a very poor part of the city, but we love being with the people. It is not easy living here. My wife and I have a small child, and we are concerned about his safety and education. We are not yet certain how that will work out.

"I don't have a job yet and am using my experience in Tibet to help me start a new business. We have to rely upon the Lord for our daily needs. Getting around the town with limited language skills, not being familiar with the foods or culture, and not having sufficient funds for long-term expenses make things more difficult.

"Simple things like water and electricity for our apartment are an answer to prayer for us, and God has never failed us. He continues to show us that He is walking together with us.

"When we first arrived here there were only a few people that I was able to share the gospel with. They received Jesus as their Lord and Savior and now there are already 25-30 students attending our fellowship.

"We pray that God's message continues to penetrate the heart of the people. We find it such a privilege to serve Him here."

THINK ABOUT IT

Many consider it an honor when they are commissioned by an earthly king, but a burden when they are commissioned by the King of kings.

Simon left his home in China when it was most inconvenient. His area of China was finally experiencing an economic boom for the first time in generations. It would have been easier to leave his hometown during the height of the Cultural Revolution, World War II, or the Japanese Occupation period. The convenience of God calling one out of that hardship would have been an easy trade-off, but to leave a home that is finally experiencing newfound prosperity seemed like insanity.

Simon does not lie about the hardships in Tibet or ignore them. He readily admits that it is not an easy place for his family, but Simon's joy is not dependent upon his circumstances. Is yours?

SCRIPTURE READING

Large crowds were traveling with Jesus. Turning to them, he said, "Whoever comes to me and doesn't hate father and mother, spouse and children, and brothers and sisters—yes, even one's own life—cannot be my disciple. Whoever doesn't carry their own cross and follow me cannot be my disciple.

Luke 14:25-27

Day 17

The Bible Man

  The Bible Man's testimony, like many of the other testimonies in this devotional, is a precious piece of the history of the Chinese House church. The Bible Man's real name was Mai Fu Ren. He passed away in 2010, but will never be forgotten by the Chinese church.

  Mai Fu Ren grew up in Southern China in a place called Shantou, which was the target destination for the first one million Bibles to ever be delivered to China in one shipment.

  The covert operation was code named "Project Pearl" and was run by a former U.S. Marine. When the team delivered the Bibles to a beach in the middle of the night in the summer of 1981, Mai Fu Ren was one of the locals there to receive them and disperse them throughout China.

  Believers all around China were fasting and

praying for a Bible in those days. When Mai Fu Ren arrived with their Bibles in hand he was considered to be an agent of the Lord. However, when the government found out about his secret work, they were not kind to him.

He shares some of his story here:

"Because the Lord healed me when I was young, my parents wanted me to serve the Lord full-time, but I told them that I didn't want to," Mai Fu Ren remembers. "I was not a Christian and didn't believe in God."

"I eventually became a Christian, but soon after that, I had my freedom taken away from me. Not for five, ten, fifteen, or even twenty years, but I was put in prison for thirty years. A thirty-year prison sentence is a difficult thing to comprehend, let alone endure.

"When I first entered into the prison, they went through all of my belongings. I had a small Bible and I hid it the best I could. None of the other things mattered to me. What mattered most was my Bible.

"I wasn't that concerned about being in prison. I knew that there were many people in the prison who needed to hear the gospel. As soon as I arrived I began to share with people.

"One prisoner asked me, 'So you are saying that Karl Marx was a sinner?'

"'Yes, Karl Marx sinned. We have all sinned and only Jesus can save us,' I replied.

"The prisoner was confused because he believed that only teaching things contrary to Karl Marx was a sin. So how could Karl Marx be a sinner? The prisoner took this to the top prison leaders and they came together and had a conference.

"After the prison conference, it was announced on the loudspeakers to everyone in the prison: 'Mai Fu Ren is an anti-revolutionary. He will have two more years added to his prison sentence for spreading anti-revolutionary teachings.'

"During the Cultural Revolution in China the government would host judgment conferences where they would condemn Christians and Christian teachings. All Bibles and Christian books would be brought to the town square and thrown into a big fire.

"I remember thinking to myself, 'Do you really think that true Christians will stop believing if you burn all of their literature? I don't think so.'"

After Mai Fu Ren got out of prison, most of his siblings had already passed away. He didn't have a life to go back to. China had changed greatly in the thirty years that he was in prison, and most of the new believers in the underground movement had never even heard of him.

"I never sought recognition. I didn't really do much, only what the Lord told me to do. It didn't take much effort to stay in prison," he said, prior to going on his first and last trip abroad to the Philippines.

When Mai Fu Ren passed away he didn't have a bank account, a large house, a college degree, or a letter of gratitude from all of the thousands of people he helped to receive a Bible, because his treasures were laid up in heaven where moth and rust cannot destroy.

THINK ABOUT IT

Sometimes the greatest challenge after experiencing a small trial is for us not to believe that we made it out because of our own greatness. Trials of death and loss tend to have the opposite effect.

How many untold thousands are saved today in China because of the Bibles that Mai Fu Ren delivered? How many lives did he touch who never knew his sacrifice of thirty years in prison?

Mai Fu Ren's value cannot be ascertained in the monetary assets that he had on the day when he passed away, but instead was judged by the King of Kings. The untold thousands of people that he helped bring into the knowledge of the Kingdom of God were added as jewels to his crown that day.

SCRIPTURE READING

Be careful that you don't practice your religion in front of people to draw their attention. If you do, you will have no reward from your Father who is in heaven. Whenever you give to the poor, don't blow your trumpet as the hypocrites do in the synagogues and in the streets so that they may get praise from people. I assure you, that's the only reward they'll get. But when you give to the poor, don't let your left hand know what your right hand is doing so that you may give to the poor in secret. Your Father who sees what you do in secret will reward you.

When you pray, don't be like hypocrites. They love

to pray standing in the synagogues and on the street corners so that people will see them. I assure you, that's the only reward they'll get. But when you pray, go to your room, shut the door, and pray to your Father who is present in that secret place. Your Father who sees what you do in secret will reward you.

Matthew 6: 1-6

** If possible, read the Next Devotion
tomorrow morning at 5 a.m. **

China's Songbird Xiao Min

Walk into any underground church service in China and you will, without a doubt, hear the songs of Xiao Min. Xiao Min has written more than one thousand traditional Chinese worship songs known as the Canaan Hymns.

Xiao Min was still a young peasant girl when the Holy Spirit began to place worship music into her soul. She dropped out of junior high school and is to this day unable to read music. She grew up in China's Henan Province to an illiterate father and a mother who had never attended school.

Living life in the farming village was not always easy, but Xiao Min would find inspiration in a Bible verse and begin singing its words with a Chinese melody. During her private time, she would sew words and lyrics together that helped her to express praise to God.

She sang the songs to herself as she walked through the rice fields. Pastor Zhang Rongliang spotted her at a home church meeting one evening and, after hearing some of her songs, immediately felt that she was able to tell the story of the Chinese persecuted church in a powerful way.

There is one song that echoes strongly within the hearts of all home church leaders in China called "China at Five in the Morning". It was recorded by Back to Jerusalem and distributed to all of the main networks in the year 2000.

"The Lord is coming back soon," Xiao Min said during one interview with the Christian Times in September 2012. "How can Christians today welcome His return? We should pray in the early morning, learn how to wait on God, love one another, be as one, live in the presence of God, and continually consecrate ourselves to his service..."

"How long should we sleep in the morning? Before Jesus comes, we should wake up early in the morning. To do what? To pray."

Brother Yun and well-known house church pastor Peter Xu have not lived in China for several years, but like the leaders who are still in China, you will find them on their knees at 5 a.m. every single morning.

THINK ABOUT IT

People often ask why the Chinese are still experiencing such a large revival after all these years. How can a revival of this magnitude have possibly been sustained for such a long time?

There are many answers given by the leaders as to why the Chinese revival has lasted for so many years, but none more universal than their early morning prayer. Wake up at 5 a.m. in any city in China and you can be assured that the majority of the underground House church Christians in that area are on their knees in passionate prayer.

The important thing to know is that prayer has not been traditionally taught about in China. Only recently have training materials been provided in the churches, but the curriculum comes from western theological textbooks. Instead, the Chinese have learned about prayer personally, by praying with other believers. The learning process takes place primarily through observation and participation.

Xiao Min's song, "China at Five in the Morning," might be one of the most famous of all her writings. This is not just because its melody is powerful, but because it captures the essence of what it means to start off the day in the way that the Chinese underground House church does every morning.

SCRIPTURE READING

Hear my words, Lord! Consider my groans! Pay attention to the sound of my cries, my king and my God, because I am praying to you! Lord, in the morning you hear my voice. In the morning I lay it all out before you. Then I wait expectantly. Because you aren't a God who enjoys wickedness; evil doesn't live with you. Arrogant people won't last long in your sight; you hate all evildoers; you destroy liars.

The Lord despises people who are violent and dishonest. But me? I will enter your house because of your abundant, faithful love; I will bow down at your holy temple, honoring you. Lord, because of many enemies, please lead me in your righteousness. Make your way clear, right in front of me. Because there's no truth in my enemies' mouths, all they have inside them is destruction. Their throats are open graves; their tongues slick with talk. Condemn them, God! Let them fail by their own plans. Throw them out for their many sins because they've rebelled against you.

But let all who take refuge in you celebrate. Let them sing out loud forever! Protect them so that all who love your name can rejoice in you. Because you, Lord, bless the righteous. You cover them with favor like a shield.

Psalm 5

Day **19**

Pastor "Little Joe"

Pastor Joe is another House church network leader in China. He is currently leading a network that was founded by his father. Little Joe works with very few foreigners; in fact, he may not work with any at all outside those partnered with Back to Jerusalem.

Little Joe first started preaching in the 1990s and began to take over the leadership of the church when his father was in prison. He had always wanted to be a preacher like his father. At the outset of his ministry, the only support he received came from his parents who were extremely poor. Naturally, a father who is habitually getting arrested is not the most ideal source of ministry funding.

Little Joe's lowest point came in 2000 when he was arrested in Anhui Province. The judge sentenced him to three years in prison for preaching the Gospel. He was sentenced to serve his three years at an infamous coal mine labor camp, the same dreaded labor camp, in fact, that his father had served in years before.

"That prison was especially hard on Christians," Little Joe recalled.

"I know that many Christians tell stories that end in wonderful testimonies about God's amazing grace and power bringing them miraculously through the most trying times, but that was not always the case for us.

"The coal mine was torture for Christians serving time there. Coal mining is one of the most dangerous and physically demanding jobs in China. [The Chinese government] likes to use Christians and political dissidents for labor in the coal mines. Many go in, but few come out. There was a brother who was in love with the Lord and was arrested in Anhui then sent to the labor camp. He was told to deny the name of the Lord. He refused and was sent to the coal mine. He was again told to deny the name of the Lord. He again refused. The guards beat him mercilessly for refusing to deny the Lord.

"Every day each prisoner in the mine has to fill a quota. If they do not complete their quota they will be punished. After the Christian brother was beaten, he was not able to complete his quota the next day. He was beaten again and kicked in the head. He was kicked so hard that it caused him serious brain damage. He was not able to bear the abuse any longer, so he used a lamp in the shower room, took the bulb out of the socket, turned on the water, and killed himself. He just couldn't take it anymore.

"Torture for a few days or even weeks might be

bearable, but when there is no end in sight, there can be times when the human body and mind just quit."

In the movie "Defiance," a Rabbi undoubtedly echoes the sentiments of countless Jews during World War II, when they were hunted like animals and starving with no place to live. The Rabbi led a small group of Jews in prayer after the death of one of their comrades while hiding in the forest. The Rabbi prayed:

We commit our friends into your hands. We have no more prayers, no more tears; we have run out of blood. Choose another people. We have paid for each of your commandments. We have covered them with headstones in the field. Sanctify another mount. Choose another people. Teach them the deeds and the prophesies. Grant us but one more blessing: Take back the gift of our holiness.

In times of our deepest suffering, it is often tempting for Christians to pray likewise, but we have a Hope that does not disappoint.

THINK ABOUT IT

Do true Christians lose the battle if believers die in prison even when they pray for release? Are they lacking in faith if they don't escape their suffering miraculously?

Furthermore, was Stephen in the Bible lacking in faith since the Lord did not protect him from the rocks thrown by the Pharisees?

The thief on the cross was never promised immediate earthly deliverance, but received eternal life in God's Kingdom by the Giver of Life. Was he cheated? Should he have received both?

These are not the easy feel-good questions that are fun to ask oneself. They are even less easy to answer for those who have lost loved ones or are suffering from persecution.

Today, try not to be too quick to formulate your answer to the above questions. Pray for wisdom from the Father as you go through your day. Pray for those who are in prison for the sake of the gospel. There are Christians in prison today in China, North Korea, Iran, and many other countries around the world. They are most likely hurting, tired, hungry, and missing their families.

Some of them might be thinking about giving up their faith. Many of them might be questioning it right now or even looking up at that light socket, even as you read these words. Pray for those suffering believers, that they may have the powerful faith of Shadrach, Meshach, and Abednego as they face their own fiery furnace.

SCRIPTURE READING

Nebuchadnezzar said to them: "Shadrach, Meshach, and Abednego: Is it true that you don't serve my gods or worship the gold statue I've set up? If you are now ready to do so, bow down and worship the gold statue I've made when you hear the sound of horn, pipe, zither, lyre, harp, flute, and every kind of instrument.

But if you won't worship it, you will be thrown straight into the furnace of flaming fire. Then what god will rescue you from my power?"

Shadrach, Meshach, and Abednego answered King Nebuchadnezzar: "We don't need to answer your question. If our God—the one we serve—is able to rescue us from the furnace of flaming fire and from your power, Your Majesty, then let him rescue us. But if he doesn't, know this for certain, Your Majesty: we will never serve your gods or worship the gold statue you've set up."

Daniel 3:14-18

Day 20

第二十回

Pastor Enguan

Very few people know anything about the churches in Anhui Province or about their history.

The leaders of Lixin Network have never approached anyone with a glossy full-color brochure about their church of five million believers. They wouldn't even think of mentioning that they are one of the five largest House church networks in China, nor that they are one of the largest church movements in all of Anhui Province with more congregants than the entire country of New Zealand.

If you do a Google search on the Lixin church, you will not find any information about its history or leadership. At the time of this writing, they most definitely do not have a Twitter account.

Finding information on the history of Lixin is not easy because, in June of 2011, the police raided its leadership meeting and confiscated all of its records.

Lixin Church, originally named after Lixin County, is also known as "Blessing Network" or "Mongfu" in Chinese.

Enguan, one of the Lixin founders, was saved in 1978 at the age of 16 and what happened next was one of the most unusual church growth stories to ever come out of China.

At the age of fourteen, Enguan's father became ill and died. Two years later his mother also became seriously ill. According to Enguan, she had also been demon possessed for a long time. His older brother had serious issues with his ears, but his family was too poor to pay for treatment. The family did not have the money to help Enguan's father when he became sick two years earlier and still did not have money to help his mother or brother.

"I believe that God used poverty to teach me to trust in Him," Enguan says as a matter of fact.

There were only six known Chinese Christians who lived in his village at that time. They were a remnant from the time of foreign missionaries, who had since departed. None of them were literate. His uncle was one of those six Christians, and he would often sing old hymns to his God, but did not have a Bible or any significant formal education.

Even though Enguan was not a Christian, he was comforted during those most trying times by hearing his uncle's songs. He asked his uncle to teach him the old hymns that he was always singing. He did not know any of the hymns in their entirety, only portions of them.

Once he had learned them from his uncle, Enguan found comfort in their words and peace in their melodies. Even before he became a Christian, he would already share the hymns with others.

He wanted to ask the Christians to come and pray for his mother because of her demon possession, but in China it is customary to feed houseguests. He didn't have any food to give them if they came to his home to pray for his mother. Since he couldn't afford rice flour, eventually he made flour out of sweet potatoes and offered it to the Christians in his village when they came over to pray.

During their visits he would listen carefully to every word that they prayed. Since he couldn't afford to keep asking them to come and pray for his mother, he memorized the words of their prayers and prayed them over her himself.

One day he knelt down and began praying for his mother, and suddenly she was set free from demon possession. All of the local Christians who heard about it rejoiced. At that time the local Christians didn't have any worship services, so Enguan began to hold meetings at his home, which became the very first House church of Lixin County. The formation of Lixin House church Network had begun.

There were other families in the area that also had members who were completely out of their minds with unexplainable madness. Word began to spread that this kind of uncontrollable behavior could be demon possession. Enguan received requests to travel around and pray for those who were demon possessed. As he prayed, people were set free from the demons and entire families came to the Lord.

Enguan did not have a Bible, thus he had no way to reference any of the prayers he was praying, nor any way to formally introduce people to the God who was setting them free from demon possession. To him Jesus was only a name that demonstrated power of deliverance and he placed his faith in the name of Jesus.

All he knew were the old hymns taught to him by the old believers In the village. Whenever there were people who needed prayer he would pray the few words that he had heard prayed before in the name of Jesus and sing the hymns. People were set free and he began to see miracles take place. It was unexplainable.

It is not easy for people from that generation to explain how things happened in those early days, but people saw the miracles and believed. They believed in Jesus as their Lord and began to call themselves Christians.

The first House church in Lixin met together in Enguan's home. It was more of a hospital for the sick than a gathering place for believers because sick people who had no other hope for treatment would travel from far away to be miraculously healed. They came because they had heard the rumors of other sick people being healed. Enguan prayed for them and many were indeed healed. This led to even more people believing and telling their friends, family, and acquaintances about the healings.

Many miracles were taking place and the church was growing, but the believers didn't have anything more than mere songs to rely on for their faith. They cherished those songs and held close to themselves the prayers in the name of Jesus that showed power to heal the sick and perform miracles, but there was no Bible to be found anywhere. No one had ever even seen a Bible or knew anyone else who had.

In the 1980s the husband of a Christian couple in that same area was seriously ill and about to die. One day his wife decided to get baptized. She believed that if she got baptized, Jesus would see her and bless the water surrounding her. She was baptized and immediately collected the water around herself in a bottle. She brought it to her sick husband and asked him to drink it. Amazingly, he drank from the water and was healed. Without a Bible there was no possible way for the people in Lixin County to understand the meaning of the miracles, but God responded to their sometimes-misguided acts of faith anyway.

After some time the people of Lixin church were finally able to get their hands on a Bible. The problem then was that they could not understand it. They were very excited to have a Bible in their midst, but were not exactly sure what to do with it, so when sick people came to their home church meetings, they would place the Bible on the bed and tell people to go into the room with the bed and place their forehead on the Bible. Again, people who were sick and did this were healed from their illness. God was gracious in their ignorance.

After the people of the Lixin Church received a Bible they employed two main methods to heal the sick. One way was to have the Bible on the bed and have the sick people lay on it. Sometimes they even used the Bible like a pillow and believed in their healing.

The second way was to hit people with the Bible. The leaders of Lixin Church would tell the sick people to stand still and would take the Bible and actually hit them on the head with it. Amazingly, both ways worked repeatedly.

"We were one of the most heavily-persecuted churches in all of China. Christians in our area were not Christians for long before they were rounded up by the police. You would meet believers who had been saved for six years and had served five and a half of those years in prison. It was not uncommon for baby Christians to only be saved for a month before being martyred for their faith. This was normal life during the early days of the Lixin Network."

In 1999 Enguan was arrested and went to jail for two years. During that time his job was to make television boxes for Haier Electronics. Pastor Enguan had access to convicts on death row and preached the gospel to them. Even though they were in the most hopeless of situations with no light at the end of the tunnel, these prisoners found love and mercy in Christ. Every prisoner on the death row of that prison became a Christian.

THINK ABOUT IT

The love of Jesus was preached through half-learned songs? The healing power of Christ was demonstrated by individuals who did not even own a Bible? God used poverty to teach a pastor about faith? A church with millions of believers exists without a Facebook page, Twitter Account, or even an advertisement in the local newspaper? Is it really possible?

SCRIPTURE READING

Heaven is declaring God's glory; the sky is proclaiming his handiwork. One day gushes the news to the next, and one night informs another what needs to be known. Of course, there's no speech, no words—their voices can't be heard—but their sound extends throughout the world; their words reach the ends of the earth.

Psalm 19:1-4

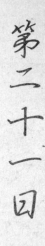

Day 21

Pastor Zhang Rongliang

On June 2, 1971 I was detained at a local jail while a small detachment of police were sent to my home to look for my Bible and any other religious writings. I knew that they would not find my Bible. I often gave it to others and we had a system of shuffling it around from one house to another to keep it from being discovered by the police. The team tore my home apart, piece by piece, searching for my Bible. They knew that I had a Bible, but I would not tell them where it was. They didn't find it, but they did find my hymnal and you would have thought that they had found a thousand Bibles by the way they acted. They were ecstatic with their discovery of the hymnal, believing that they had found a sacred treasure. They proceeded to recommend that I be prosecuted in front of the judge for owning an illegal book. Even though I knew that a hymnal is not the same as a

Bible, to the Party officials it was just as incriminating.

A short time earlier, there was an older Christian of retirement age who was heard singing Christian songs of praise by himself. The Party official who heard him asked what he was singing about. When the old gentleman explained the song to him, the official asked, "Do you hate socialism? Hasn't the Communist Party treated you well? Are you trying to engage in class warfare?" The man was reported to the authorities and was eventually sentenced to four years in a re-education camp. If he received a four-year sentence just for singing a song, I thought they might want to give me the death penalty since they found an entire hymnal in my possession.

When the search party returned to the jail, they had my hymnal in their hands. They waved it around and showed the others their prized treasure.

"Where did you get this?" they demanded as they looked at me. "Who gave you this song book?"

"No one gave it to me. I wrote the songs in that book."

"I don't think so. You couldn't have written the songs in this book. You are too stupid. You didn't even finish school. You can barely read, let alone write songs!"

I was sent to a private cell where they continued to question me, "Where did you get that book? Who gave it to you? Who is distributing this illegal contraband?"

I didn't answer, but I was becoming hungry because they had quit feeding me several days earlier. They were deliberately depriving me of food so that I would be more apt to break. First food deprivation, then sleep deprivation. I knew how things were going to be, but that didn't make it any easier.

Communism does something very cruel to a person. It takes away the personalization of individuals. In fact, any social institution that systematically removes belief in God does this. Christians understand that we are brothers and sisters in Christ Jesus. We are a family. We even recognize that non-believers are created in the image of God. We have the Golden Rule, "Do to others as you would have them do to you." In Christ Jesus it is not permissible to torture others because true Christians would be conscious of a reversal of roles. It is not possible for a Christian to look into the eyes of a torture victim and not empathize with them even to the point of flinching with each blow.

Atheist communism takes away that shared commonality. People are no longer people. They are not thought of as sons and daughters, mothers and fathers, or brothers and sisters, but are seen as a collective machine-like workforce that needs to produce more than it consumes. People are also devalued to the point of animals in accordance with evolutionary theories.

In Communist China, people are expendable. Every day my captors interrogated me. I kept getting weaker from a lack of food. The guards would beat me to the ground and then kick me. Every blow seemed to jolt my entire body more and more as I weakened from hunger. They were losing patience and I was losing consciousness.

On the third day of beatings, my frail body was exhausted and depleted of sustenance. The summer heat was inescapable. There was no bed and it was hard for me to sleep on the floor. I tried to find the coolest place on the floor to lie down in order to keep from sweating. I knew that the more I sweat, the more dehydrated I would become, but eventually I was too weak to care.

"Why are you doing this Zhang?" The guards would ask me. "Why can't you just give up your foolish beliefs and work with us?"

What could I say? How could I help them understand that the love of Jesus is greater than any love we might experience in this world?

I didn't want to be tortured anymore, but I knew that if I lost my Bible I might never get another one. I thought of dear Grandfather Sun who had given it to me and of the words that he had shared with me before he was martyred.

"Zhang, you must live and die with that Bible. No matter what, you must not allow them to take it from you," I told myself. That Bible was my life. It was a family treasure and I knew I had to guard it and keep it safe. I never told them where my Bible was and they never found it. Praise God.

THINK ABOUT IT

Would it take a police force to separate you from your Bible or would a good movie do the trick?

SCRIPTURE READING

The words of Agur, Jakeh's son, from Massa. The man declares: I'm tired, God; I'm tired, God, and I'm exhausted. Actually, I'm too stupid to be human, a man without understanding. I haven't learned wisdom, nor do I have knowledge of the holy one. Who has gone up to heaven and come down? Who has gathered the wind by the handful? Who has bound up the waters in a garment? Who has established all the ends of the earth? What is this person's name and the name of this person's child—if you know it?

All God's words are tried and true; a shield for those who take refuge in him. Don't add to his words, or he will correct you and show you to be a liar.

Two things I ask of you; don't keep them from me before I die: Fraud and lies—keep far from me! Don't give me either poverty or wealth; give me just the food I need. Or I'll be full and deny you, and say, "Who is the Lord?" Or I'll be poor and steal, and dishonor my God's name.

Proverbs 30:1-10

Day 22

Brother Jacob

Brother Jacob is another evangelist from Mongfu (Lixin) Church, also known as the Blessing Network. He is 23 years old today and had only been a Christian for less than two years before he was sent out as an evangelist. He had been serving in his area of ministry for less than 10 months when he gave the following report:

"I was sent by my leader to be a full-time worker in Xincheng County. There were Christians in that county whom I was able to connect with, but there was also a strong feeling of division and oppression in the area.

"I did not know how to help the people there. I was at a complete loss of what I could do to make their lives better and prayed that God would send someone to guide me. I felt ill-equipped to help in any way, so I prayed, but received no immediate answers.

"I connected with the only believers that I had heard about in the county and when I went to their home to meet with them I found that they were all older. When we came together I learned that the Christian families in the area were under a full-scale spiritual attack. All the older women in the fellowship were married to men who were not serving the Lord and were abusive to their families.

"I asked that all of us come together every day for prayer at five in the morning. On the first morning we started praying and didn't stop until late that afternoon. The people were expecting me to preach to them, but I felt the Lord urging us all to continue praying.

"The next day we did the same thing. We prayed from five in the morning until four or five in the afternoon. On that second day we experienced a breakthrough in the Spirit. Our hearts opened up and poured out before the Lord. All of our transgressions, worries, fears and problems were confessed before the Lord and true repentance came flowing out of us.

"'Jesus is our Lord. Jesus is the Lord over our family. He is the Master of our lives. Are we willing to submit to our Master and King?'

"I felt the power of the Lord well up in me as I cried out the message in passionate prayer: "The Lord wants to change our situations, but how can you expect Him to control something that you are holding onto yourselves? Can we make Jesus the Lord over only our problems? Can we make Jesus the Master over only our mistakes? Submit everything to the King. Submit everything to the Master."

"I looked at each person individually, and while I was still in the spirit of prayer I asked them: 'Are you willing to give everything to Him? Are you willing to submit to the King of Kings? Are you willing to give over your life to His control?'

"Everyone was sobbing and nodding their heads in affirmation. We had a major breakthrough that day and we saw things start to change almost immediately. Husbands began to come and join us. They started to show affection to their wives. Some of the wives had already been divorced, but now they shared testimonies about remarrying their husbands. Families were being restored and husbands and wives were falling in love again. One woman whose husband had left her because she was not able to have a baby for nine years was reunited with her husband and became pregnant.

"Another woman was not able to tithe because her husband was so far in debt. They always fought over financial problems, but their marriage was restored and soon they were able to clear all of their debts.

"God has performed many miracles in the last several months among our families even though we did not know the proper way to come to Him. The Bible tells us to first seek the Kingdom of God and that is all we did.

THINK ABOUT IT

How simple is the testimony of Brother Jacob?! Think about the lives that were changed even though his fellowship didn't have a church building, administrative office, registration center, denomination, licensed therapists, or sign-up fees.

The underground church in China is not changing lives because it is growing. It is growing because lives are being changed.

SCRIPTURE READING

"Therefore, don't worry and say, 'What are we going to eat?' or 'What are we going to drink?' or 'What are we going to wear?' Gentiles long for all these things. Your heavenly Father knows that you need them. Instead, desire first and foremost God's kingdom and God's righteousness, and all these things will be given to you as well. Therefore, stop worrying about tomorrow, because tomorrow will worry about itself. Each day has enough trouble of its own."

Matthew 6:31-34

Brother Joshua

Joshua is one of the main "uncles" in an underground House church network that does not have a name. Because it doesn't have a proper name, it is often referred to as the "No Name" network. This network is led by five main leaders who share the authority over a group of several million believers. Joshua is one of the uncles who manage the day-to-day operations of the network churches under the authority of the five leaders.

"Many people learn about Back to Jerusalem but are not really sure how they fit into the vision," Joshua said to a church on his second trip to America. "The Back to Jerusalem vision is not just a task for the Chinese. It is a commission that has been given to the church of this day. It includes all people."

"When I read the book of Exodus, I see a story that

has much to teach us about the Back to Jerusalem vision.

"After the Israelites had been slaves for several hundred years, they cried out to God and He heard their cries. Their days of suffering in slavery were coming to an end and they were going to be led into the land that God had promised their ancestors—the land of milk and honey.

"But leaving slavery was not an easy task. The Israelites continued to suffer, challenge after challenge. From the first day that they left Egypt they were walking on a road that they had never walked on before. They were going in a direction that none of them had ever traveled before. Traveling in unknown territory with an entire nation is not easy, especially when traversing the unforgiving desert.

"As soon as the Israelites were out of danger from the Egyptians in a place called Rephidim, another enemy rose up and attacked them. This didn't seem like a good deal at all to them. Did God deliver the Israelites out of Egypt only to throw them into war?

"They were looking for the land of milk and honey; they were not looking for a war. However, war is what they got when Amalek attacked them.

"Moses, Aaron, and Hur did not lead the Isrealites onto the battlefield. Instead, they went to the top of a hill. The Israelites already did not know what they were supposed to be doing and now even their most senior leader was on top of a hill, holding up a stick.

"Have you ever thought about how dangerous this was, sending an untrained army to the battlefield under a leader with zero experience?

"In China, we have been taken from the frying pan of persecution and sent to the battlefield of Muhammed and Buddha. We have been led out of the slavery of Communism into the battle of Animism and Hinduism and God is calling the leadership in China to go up to the mountain and pray.

"It is not enough to have the vision of Back to Jerusalem. The vision alone is not a guarantor of victory. God commands our leadership to go up to the high places and to pray over the army that is being sent out. God never commanded us to establish a committee that could utilize the best minds to strategize how the battle plan will unfold. God never commissioned us to find the most intellectually feasible way to gather souls from the harvest. We need to seek after Him in prayer and fasting.

"Why do we have to go to the mountain? So that we can hear what the Lord is saying in our specific situation. Intellect will fail us. People are looking for answers and asking why China is having a revival when they are not. The answer is very simple. The leadership in China is fervently seeking after God in prayer."

THINK ABOUT IT

"It is not enough to have vision." How many times have we grown comfortable with only having a vision? How many times have we settled for good intentions?

SCRIPTURE READING

"Don't fear, because I am with you; don't be afraid, for I am your God. I will strengthen you, I will surely help you; I will hold you with my righteous strong hand.

"All who rage against you will be shamed and disgraced. Those who contend with you will be as nothing and will perish. You will look for your opponents, and won't find them. Those who fight you will be of no account and will die. I am the Lord your God, who grasps your strong hand, who says to you, don't fear; I will help you."

Isaiah 41:10-13

Brother Yun

"One day God spoke to my heart and told me to travel to Greece to plant a church there. I had never been to Greece, and I didn't have any contacts in Greece. I contacted everyone I knew to see if they had any friends there. I don't speak English or Greek, so it would be difficult to travel there by myself. I had every reason not to go, but God had put the country on my heart and I knew better than to refuse His calling.

"I boarded a plane with my wife and within only a hours of our arrival God God connected me with some Chinese who were living in the city of Athens. I traveled to a factory and to a retail shop and in both places I met young people who were living with people all around them, but who were lonely inside. With the permission of the business owners, I spoke about the love of Jesus with the workers. Within minutes, the young people began to cry and several of them gave their hearts to Christ.

"I was petitioned to travel to the local jail and to minister to a young lady who was an incarcerated illegal immigrant. Miraculously, although I wasn't even a citizen of the country, the police handed her over to my custody. Together we were able to start a small fellowship of new believers that is still thriving today in that business place."

Brother Yun continued his story in Seattle, Washington in 2013, "When Jesus or the disciples performed miracles, healed the sick, or preached the Gospel, the majority of the time it was not in the temple, but instead on the streets, in homes, and in other public areas." Brother Yun then exhorted his listeners to be disciples of Jesus instead of merely comfortable Christians getting fat in churches without ever living their lives outside the insulation of insurance.

"You don't need miracles in the West. You have insurance. You have insurance for your car, your house, and your health, and many Christians view Jesus as just another insurance plan. You don't want to go to hell so you get 'Jesus insurance' and just acknowledge Him enough to get into heaven."

Brother Yun lives in Germany and his children are German citizens. Germany and Greece are currently at odds over economic issues, but Brother Yun believes strongly in blessing those who are against you.

Shortly after leaving China, Brother Yun was strongly attacked by other Christian believers around the world. Ministry websites and newsletters attacked his story and his character. Instead of retaliating, Brother Yun prayed for them.

China tortured him and threw him into prison to die. Today he refuses to openly attack or protest against the government of China or to say anything that would be disparaging toward the current regime.

In the fall of 2013, Brother Yun traveled around the United States on a "Bless Your Enemies" tour. Few places in the world are more dangerous than the countries between China and Jerusalem where Chinese missionaries are being sent today.

Back to Jerusalem missionaries are currently focused on China, North Korea, and Iran. Iran is a religious theocracy run by an Islamic Ayatollah who has posed a continual threat to the rest of the world for decades. North Korea is a closed-off Communist country that continues to kill its own people and to threaten its neighbors.

Human rights are being abused, Christians are being tortured, and Israel is being threatened. The international community is continually challenged by the danger that these countries pose to the rest of the world and their neighbors and are rendered helpless.

World leaders are constantly looking for a solution to neutralize the threat that they pose. Should we impose economic sanctions? Should the UN write a strongly worded letter to them? Should we send in troops? Should we drop bombs?

The international community has collectively spent billions of dollars on expert consultants, intelligence, diplomatic negotiations, and military posturing, but nothing seems to work. The world is no safer from the Iranian or North Korean threat than it was before. In fact, many argue that the threats are getting worse. After billions of dollars and the smartest experts on the planet, the world is still not even one step closer to a peaceful solution in regard to these hostile nations.

Two thousand years ago Christ gave his followers a simple solution to the inevitable conflict that they would face in their lives: "But I say to you, love your enemies, bless them that curse you, do good to them that hate you, and pray for them which despitefully use you, and persecute you."

What if we sent missionaries instead of troops to the most hostile areas in the world? What if we sent them Bibles instead of bombs?

THINK ABOUT IT

Jesus promised that serving Him would earn us enemies, but at the same time we were told to love them. This seems like self-imposed torture. Following Jesus will make for us more enemies than friends, and yet we are commanded to cover them with love and prayers.

How far would you go to show love to your enemies? Could it be that our enemies today might be our brothers and sisters of tomorrow?

SCRIPTURE READING

Keep the belief that you have to yourself—it's between you and God. People are blessed who don't convict themselves by the things they approve. But those who have doubts are convicted if they go ahead and eat, because they aren't acting on the basis of faith. Everything that isn't based on faith is sin.

Romans 17:22-23

Day **25**

Sister Grace He

The Back to Jerusalem vision is not a new vision. It was birthed in the hearts of Chinese believers in the early 1900s. One of the first groups to catch the vision was the Back to Jerusalem Evangelistic Band.

Sister Grace He, one of its original members, passed away in January 2014. Here is a shortened version of her personal testimony:

In the year 1942 I arrived in Shaanxi with Pastor Mark Ma and Brother Zhang. During the spring of 1943 we were still there and decided to attend an Easter Service in Baoji. Mountains surrounded the church, so we had to leave early to arrive on time to the Easter sunrise service.

As the sun started to come up and we were

walking along the mountain ridges, I thought of the first Easter morning when Mary Magdalene came upon the tomb only to find that it was empty. In that moment I was also reminded of my own testimony.

When I was about fifteen years old I was first living in Tianjin and then in Beijing. At that time, I had a very vivid vision of a map and on that map was a large sea with a tiny boat. The sea was roaring and the boat was being tossed about. The tiny boat was at the mercy of the gusting winds and tempest.

"That tiny boat is you," a voice said to me.

"Me?" I asked.

Immediately I was filled with fear and began to pray. "Dear Heavenly Father, I pray for your protection. Don't remove me from your safety and peace."

I was praying, but I still felt fear. I was praying in the way that I had been taught. My mother prompted us to pray every evening. She taught us exactly how to pray and what to say. If we prayed incorrectly, my mother would stop us and tell us that bad things would happen if we didn't pray the correct way, so I naturally had fear when I prayed to God as a young girl.

I continued to pray and said, "Lord, I am afraid." Even as I prayed I could see the boat being tossed by the sea and it was adding to my fear.

"Dear Lord, look at me." And I could hear Him telling me to give my life over to him. "Lord, you know that since I was little I have prayed to you and have always followed you. What are you talking about? I am not a bad person. I am a good person who is following you and praying to you."

But the Lord spoke and said, "I knew your mother, but I don't know you." God was not satisfied with my prayers alone. I was a sinner who prayed, not a believer who sinned. My heart had never been washed clean. I prayed the way that I had been taught out of fear, but not out of acknowledgement of God's deliverance. I really didn't think that I had any sin to be forgiven of.

"I am a sinner," I said, out of amazement. At that moment, I was forced to examine my heart. I cried out, "Dear God, I had never thought about it before. I have never confessed my sins to you. I have never personally asked you to come into my heart. Lord, forgive me." I confessed my sins to Him and a powerful joy filled my soul. I felt clean and free and couldn't stop giggling with joy.

After I prayed, I ran and told my Bible teacher, "Teacher! Teacher! I am filled with joy. Look at me. The Lord has forgiven me of my sins. I have been forgiven of my sins."

"Of course you have," he responded flip-pantly.

"NO! NO! You don't understand. Now I am REALLY clean. I am no longer a fake. Before I had never really asked for forgiveness of my sins, but now it is different. I am clean. Now that God has come into my heart, I no longer have fear."

I never prayed the same after that day.

THINK ABOUT IT

Grace suffered from a spiritual disease that is not yet very common in China. She thought that she was a Christian because she had been raised as a Christian. She prayed to God and read the Bible, but only in obedience to what she had been taught by her mother, as many children do. However, a day came when she had to make the decision for herself whether she was going to receive Jesus into her heart, and it was revealed to her that God doesn't have any grandchildren.

Spiritual apathy can often be linked to cultural Christianity where one's identity, language, and comfort zone are linked to religious practices and ceremonies. This cultural connection to Christianity is often indica-tive of falsely identifying other cultural Christian prac-tices as being inferior, wrong, or even blasphemous. Passionate devotions that are unfamiliar to cultural Christians can be easily dismissed as unbiblical. Because of this worldview, some even see the House church in China as a temporary necessity during times of persecution, but expect that it will rightly "grow" into a brick and mortar church once China opens up. Are you a captive of cultural Christianity?

SCRIPTURE READING

"I know your works. You are neither cold nor hot. I wish that you were either cold or hot. So because you are lukewarm, and neither hot nor cold, I'm about to spit you out of my mouth. After all, you say, 'I'm rich, and I've grown wealthy, and I don't need a thing.' You don't realize that you are miserable, pathetic, poor, blind, and naked. My advice is that you buy gold from me that has been purified by fire so that you may be rich, and white clothing to wear so that your nakedness won't be shamefully exposed, and ointment to put on your eyes so that you may see. I correct and discipline those whom I love. So be earnest and change your hearts and lives. Look! I'm standing at the door and knocking. If any hear my voice and open the door, I will come in to be with them, and will have dinner with them, and they will have dinner with me."

Revelation 3:15-20

Day **26**

Sister An

Sister An is serving as one of the main trainers for Back to Jerusalem's Dove Project. Dove has been used to train more than 250,000 Sunday School teacher-trainers in China, Vietnam, India, Egypt, Pakistan, Ethiopia, Slovakia, Finland, Sweden, and Norway.

The program is the first of its kind because it was designed in China for the Chinese, but after hearing about its powerful effectiveness, many other churches around the world asked for its curriculum to be taught to their children's ministry leaders as well.

An is from Henan Province where Norwegian missionary Marie Monsen spent most of her time ministering in the early 1900s. Marie Monsen served in Tanghe and Fangcheng and is considered by many to be the matriarch of the house churches in Henan Province. The Chinese feel indebted to Marie Monsen and therefore felt a strong desire to send Chinese Back to Jerusalem missionaries to minister in Norway.

Sister An's leadership knew that she had a strong desire to serve as a missionary, and she was their first choice for this task. An was accustomed to the Chinese House church way in which her pastor, like most pastors in the House church, chooses where she will live, where she will serve, how much money she will make, and even whom she will marry. Arranged marriages are common in the House church, since they still play a prominent part in Chinese culture, and the pastors play a critical role in this practice.

Western minds understand the calling of God to be something very much more personal, but the majority of House church missionaries working with Back to Jerusalem submits to their leadership and waits to be sent out by their church to the most needy areas.

Sister An did not know that her leaders were planning to send her to preach the Gospel in Northern Norway.

"I really had a desire to go somewhere to serve the poor," An explains. "I didn't know where that would be. I really thought that I would end up somewhere in Africa. My heart leaped with excitement every time I thought about Africa and about sharing the Good News of Jesus with the people there.

"When my leadership told me that it was time to go, I was put on an airplane and sent out. No one told me where I was going and what I would be doing."

In China it is very common for missionaries to be sent out to other countries without actually being told where their final destination will be. Because of security concerns in China, clear and concise communication is a risk that many church leaders are not willing to take. This lack of information requires a level of discipline and devotion from Chinese missionaries that is rarely seen around the world.

"I was really ready to work among the poor. When I realized that I was going to be flying to a place called Norway, I didn't know what to think. I didn't know where Norway was. I had never flown internationally before and didn't know what I would be doing, who I would be connecting with, or even how I was going to catch my connecting flight.

"I had a boyfriend in China whom I really did not want to leave. I wanted to be with him and stay where he was. When I was told that I was being sent out as a missionary to another country, I felt the pain of saying goodbye, but knew that I must obey and carry out the mission of the Lord.

"I traveled to Norway and lived there for about two years, serving as a missionary. The time of adjustment was not easy, but God brought me through. When I arrived back in China I heard that my boyfriend had married and was no longer attending church. God knew what I needed more than I did."

An continues to travel around the world training Sunday School teachers. Her personal testimony of how she was rejected by her family for accepting Jesus Christ is moving and emotional. Her devotion is exemplary, even among the Chinese.

THINK ABOUT IT

How deeply should a person devote themselves to the mission field? How much power should a Christian leader have over your life?

Would you be willing to submit your life's plans to your church leadership and to be sent anywhere that they deemed necessary? Would you be willing to accept that the leaders of your church will choose your husband or wife?

There is no doubt room in this system for abuse, but do you think that the amazing revivals that are taking place in China have anything to do with this mindset that is engrained in the Chinese believers?

Such a strong devotion to duty and absolute loyalty might evoke visions of cult-like gatherings in the minds of independent western thinkers, but for the Chinese, it goes hand in hand with honor and commitment. Honor and commitment are the purest expressions of love. Self-sacrifice is at its very core.

Before judging the Chinese, ask yourself how this mindset is different from the way that you live your life. Then ask yourself how your life is different from the Judaic biblical culture and compare to see what similarities exist between the Chinese Christians today and the Hebrew culture in the Old Testament.

Are you willing to look up to Christ in prayer and say, "Tell me to be anything, Lord, and I will be that?"

SCRIPTURE READING

Therefore, I have a request for the elders among you. (I ask this as a fellow elder and a witness of Christ's sufferings, and as one who shares in the glory that is about to be revealed.) I urge the elders: Like shepherds, tend the flock of God among you. Watch over it. Don't shepherd because you must, but do it voluntarily for God. Don't shepherd greedily, but do it eagerly. Don't shepherd by ruling over those entrusted to your care, but become examples to the flock. And when the chief shepherd appears, you will receive an unfading crown of glory. In the same way, I urge you who are younger: accept the authority of the elders. And everyone, clothe yourselves with humility toward each other. God stands against the proud, but he gives favor to the humble.

Therefore, humble yourselves under God's power so that he may raise you up in the last day. Throw all your anxiety onto him, because he cares about you. Be clearheaded. Keep alert. Your accuser, the devil, is on the prowl like a roaring lion, seeking someone to devour. Resist him, standing firm in the faith. Do so in the knowledge that your fellow believers are enduring the same suffering throughout the world. After you have suffered for a little while, the God of all grace, the one who called you into his eternal glory in Christ Jesus, will himself restore, empower, strengthen, and establish you. To him be power forever and always. Amen.

1 Peter 5:1-11

Day 27

Sister Li

Sister Li is a Chinese Back to Jerusalem missionary. She was a seasoned worker in a church in Liaoning, in the northeastern part of China, and was newly married. One morning when she was praying, the Holy Spirit came upon her and told her clearly, "My daughter, I want you to go to Tibet."

Upon hearing the command, Sister Li became frightened. She wanted to serve the Lord and to help fulfill the Back to Jerusalem vision, but she also wanted remain under the umbrella of the support group in Shenyang.

"God," she began to pray. "I know that you are telling me to go to Tibet, but I was only married three weeks ago. I am willing to serve you here in Shenyang, but I CANNOT go to Tibet."

For the next three weeks, Sister Li was disturbed

during her prayer time. She was in toil with the command that God had given to her.

One day Sister Li decided to make a deal with God. She told God that she would first introduce the idea to her husband and let him help her make her decision. She knew that her husband would not like the idea and felt that this would provide her with a great excuse to not leave for Tibet.

When she approached her husband, he immediately refused to go.

"The Tibetans hate us Han Chinese," he yelled. "There is no way I am going to Tibet. If you go, then you will go alone. There is no future for our marriage if you leave for Tibet."

Sister Li felt that the matter was settled, but again she heard God tell her to go to Tibet and preach the Gospel. One morning after prayer she pulled out a pen and paper and wrote one of the most heartbreaking letters that she had ever written.

In the letter she tearfully told her husband that she had to go to Tibet. She would speedily complete the task that God had given to her and quickly return to him again. Once she finished the letter, she bought a ticket on the next train to Lhasa.

Once she arrived in Lhasa she realized that she didn't have a clue about what she was supposed to do. She began to walk the distance between the main square and the Potala, praying. "Well....God....I am here. What now?"

As she was praying she walked by a pile of what seemed to be burlap blankets. At the bottom of the blankets she saw a hand that was reaching out, begging for money. As Sister Li walked by, God told her to turn around and to go give the person under the blankets a hug. Sister Li didn't feel comfortable. What if it was a man under that pile of blankets? That would not be good.

Finally, she walked back, lifted up the dusty blankets, and held out her arms to embrace the person underneath. As the person began to emerge from the coverings, Sister Li was surprised to see a young lady who was severely disfigured. Her face and arms had been eaten away by leprosy.

The woman was deeply ashamed of her appearance and astounded that someone would want to hug her. Four years prior, the woman had been forced out of her village. She traveled to Lhasa to find food. She came into the city at night so that no one would know that she had leprosy and covered her entire body as she begged for money.

Now she stood there on the street, hugging Sister Li. Her open sores and raw disfigured flesh were exposed for everyone to see. Sister Li asked her to come and live with her, and soon found accommodation for the two of them. Every day she fed her patient, applied ointment to her sores, and prayed with her.

A few weeks later, as the woman was waking up in the morning, she suddenly screamed out. Sister Li ran into the room to see what had happened. As she entered the room she could hear the woman exclaiming, "I am healed! I am healed!"

There were no signs of the woman's leprosy! She had been completely healed and believed that Jesus had healed her.

She wanted to return immediately to the village that had forced her out four years ago. Sister Li traveled with her to the small village, and as they arrived there, the people came out of their homes and were amazed that there were no signs of leprosy on the woman at all.

Together Sister Li and the woman shared about the wonderful things that Jesus had done and on that first day, 22 people in a rural village in Tibet gave their lives to Christ.

THINK ABOUT IT

Sister Li exposed herself to a potentially fatal disease without a health plan in place. How would it have been different if she had just placed some spare change into the open hand on the street and walked away? When we donate money to the poor, are we truly sharing in the burden of others or are we sometimes merely making a poor attempt at appeasing a guilty conscience?

SCRIPTURE READING

"Everybody who hears these words of mine and puts them into practice is like a wise builder who built a house on bedrock. The rain fell, the floods came, and the wind blew and beat against that house. It didn't fall because it was firmly set on bedrock. But everybody who hears these words of mine and doesn't put them into practice will be like a fool who built a house on sand. The rain fell, the floods came, and the wind blew and beat against that house. It fell and was completely destroyed."

Matthew 7:24-27

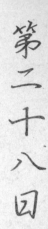

Day 28

Sister Ruth

Sister Ruth was in her early 20s when she was sent to the Philippines to be trained as a Back to Jerusalem missionary. She was very skinny, frail, and used to urban life in China. She had never traveled outside of China before and was extremely timid. Her voice was barely audible and sounded like a whisper when she talked. She easily became winded from short hikes up the most subtle of inclines. She didn't know that the Back to Jerusalem training center, set in the deep jungles of a remote Filipino island, was going to test her in ways that she had never been tested before.

The Back to Jerusalem school in the Philippines is not a typical missionary training center. It was selected as a place to provide Chinese missionaries with exposure to serving in a foreign land. It gives the Chinese a chance to work in a country that has a different culture, language, and history than their own. The Philippines is an ideal location for training missionaries because it is a Catholic country, open for preaching the Gospel. In the Philippines Chinese missionaries have the opportunity to work with militant Muslims, Buddhists, Atheists, and Animists.

Like most other Back to Jerusalem training centers, the facility in the Philippines is very atypical. The concept is based on the first century church. Students are provided with a strong practical mission focus that includes a brief introduction to the local minority mountain tribes, some practical guidelines, and hands-on evangelism experience in those areas. The Chinese live in the villages, preach the gospel, and work with the locals for a week or more before returning to the classroom. Upon their return they dissect what they did, saw, and experienced. They also discuss which strategies worked and which ones did not and are then sent back to the "bush" to minister to the same villagers a week later.

One evening of Ruth's training was unlike any other. She did not know it, but she was going to be subjected to interrogation by a former US Marine.

None of the leaders in China had been told about the specifics of the training for fear that too much prior information might compromise the element of surprise. None of the curriculum materials even alluded to the fact that the students would be put through a surprise interrogation. Ruth therefore had no idea that the interrogation was merely another "topic" within her missions training course.

With the assistance of former Filipino police officers. Ruth was awakened in the middle of the night and escorted to another building where she was asked to sit in an empty room. The interrogation training curriculum that Ruth was about to go through had been compiled by a former US Marine and a member of the US Army Special Forces, in collaboration with former Chinese House church prisoners.

Secret cameras were set up to record the entire event. Everyone was prepared for the eventual emotional roller coaster that Ruth was bound to experience. The interrogation officers were told to go easy with Ruth, since her general appearance and demeanor indicated fragility and brittleness, but no one could have expected what happened next.

Ruth was brought into the interrogation room and shown to a chair in the middle of the room where she was told to sit. As soon as she spotted the cameras facing the empty chair, she turned and walked over to the interrogator's chair.

"No, please ma'am, sit here," indicated the officer, showing her where she needed to sit for adequate filming.

"No, I am fine," she said as she stood up and led the interrogator by the hand to sit in the empty seat instead. No matter how hard the interrogator tried, he was not able to convince Ruth to sit where she was supposed to sit. Ruth did not know it, but her fellow classmate had just been interrogated in the same manner prior to her being woken up. He was a strong fellow, but did exactly as he was told.

Ruth had gone from being a timid little mouse to

a confident and persuasive young woman. The interrogators quickly took on the roles of "good cop" and "bad cop" to get Ruth to talk. She was asked questions about the Back to Jerusalem vision and the nature of her underground House church work.

Every five minutes one of the officers would leave the room and be handed a new piece of paper or incriminating photo with the next line of questions. The first questions were mainly set up to allow Ruth to incriminate herself. The questioning eventually became progressively more informed and more intrusive. As the questions grew more intense, Ruth began to make signals of having to go to the bathroom.

"Can I go to the restroom," she asked.

"No," the interrogators replied.

It was obvious that she really needed to use the restroom, but the interrogators wanted to use her situation to their advantage in order to extract more information from her. As she waited to use the restroom, she took every question and turned it around on the interrogators in the nicest, sweetest way. Her sweet words and demeanor masked her clever tenacity.

As the night turned to dawn, it became clear that the interrogation was not going as expected. Ruth was not in tears. Instead, it was the interrogators who were dismayed.

When she was told to relax and was informed that everything that she had just experienced was only for training purposes, she breathed a huge sigh of relief. So did the interrogators.

"You can use the toilet now," said one of the

trainers.

"I don't have to use the toilet," she said softly. "I just made that up so that I could make a run for it."

THINK ABOUT IT

Which Bible school have you heard of that runs courses for the students by putting them through interrogation? What would be the use of such training? Why are the Chinese churches training their workers differently than Bible schools in the West? Could it have anything to do with the countries that their missionaries are going to?

SCRIPTURE READING

"Look, I'm sending you as sheep among wolves. Therefore, be wise as snakes and innocent as doves. Watch out for people—because they will hand you over to councils and they will beat you in their synagogues. They will haul you in front of governors and even kings because of me so that you may give your testimony to them and to the Gentiles. Whenever they hand you over, don't worry about how to speak or what you will say, because what you can say will be given to you at that moment. You aren't doing the talking, but the Spirit of my Father is doing the talking through you. Brothers and sisters will hand each other over to be executed. A father will turn his child in. Children will defy their parents and have them executed. Everyone will hate you on account of my name. But whoever stands firm until the end will be saved. Whenever they harass you in one city, escape to the next, because I assure that you will not go through all the cities of Israel before the Human One comes."

Matthew 10:16-23

Day 29

Sister Jing

Shandong Province has played a pivotal role in China's revival. The Back to Jerusalem vision caught fire in that area prior to the Communist revolution. Missionaries from the West gave their lives in Shandong to bring the gospel message to the Chinese. One of those missionaries was a leading Baptist-philanthropist-turned-Pentecostal-evangelist, L.M. Aglin. A young man by the name of Jing Dianying went to work for Leslie M. Aglin, received the Lord, and was baptized in the power of the Holy Spirit.

Jing Dianying was the founder of the Jesus Family, one of the first groups to embrace the Back to Jerusalem vision.

One evening in 2006 in Guizhou several people from the hospital staff in Liupan Shui gathered together and listened to a story about the vision of Back to Jerusalem.

For three hours government officials, hospital staff, and representatives listened for the first time about this amazing vision of the Chinese underground House church. Eventually, one elderly lady in the back stood up.

"You don't know who I am," she began, "but I am the granddaughter of Jing Dianying, the founder of the Jesus Family. I can remember when I was a little girl. I saw my father and grandfather arrested for preaching the gospel. I saw my family members sent to concentration camps by the Communists. I saw my mother abandoned by the Chinese community with no way of getting a job or feeding us children. I was not allowed to go to school. I was treated like a leper. Because of what my family was I was punished by society.

"I held animosity in my heart because of what my father and grandfather had done to me. I never chose to be a Christian, and I never wanted to be a follower of Jesus Christ. It was imposed upon me by my family and now I had to suffer for something that I was born into. I felt like a trapped animal and I blamed it all on my grandfather and father.

"I told myself that I would never allow that to happen to my children. I vowed to follow the law of China to the very letter. Eventually I moved away from Shandong Province and married a government official. If I attended church, I only attended the government sanctioned church.

"But here I am tonight," she continued, "and listening to the vision of Back to Jerusalem! I am hearing the same exact words that I remember my father and grandfather saying so many years ago. The government may have killed my father and my grandfather. They may have tortured their families, but they couldn't kill the vision! They did everything they could within their power and may have felt like they had succeeded, but this is living proof that they failed. The vision of the Church in China still burns deep and even though I have denied it for most of my life, it still runs through my veins."

Her old frail frame stood erect as her voice raised in crescendo: "Though I may be old and have already wasted so many years, I promise from this day forth that I will not remain silent any longer. One more day shall not pass by without me sharing the Good News of Jesus Christ with everyone I can!"

THINK ABOUT IT

Sister Jing held on to tragic memories of her childhood. Those memories brought her pain and hatred toward her father and grandfather. She blamed them for the problems she had experienced and truly felt that Christianity was forced upon her.

However, the vision did not stop. Back to Jerusalem did not end just because Sister Jing chose to ignore it or because her father and grandfather died.

Sister Jing did not author the vision and she could not remove its power. God gives us all an important part to play in His work, but the fulfillment of His Word does not rest on our acceptance or obedience. The hate that Sister Jing harbored in her heart caused her to miss out on the plan that God had for her early life, but it was not too late for her to follow His will.

The Great Commission has been given to us all. Everyone has an important part to play in it. Which of us will, like Sister Jing, realize our role in the Great Commission prior to our passing?

SCRIPTURE READING

This is why you must make every effort to add moral excellence to your faith; and to moral excellence, knowledge; and to knowledge, self-control; and to self-control, endurance; and to endurance, godliness; and to godliness, affection for others; and to affection for others, love. If all these are yours and they are growing in you, they'll keep you from becoming inactive and unfruitful in the knowledge of our Lord Jesus Christ. Whoever lacks these things is shortsighted and blind, forgetting that they were cleansed from their past sins.

Therefore, brothers and sisters, be eager to confirm your call and election. Do this and you will never ever be lost. In this way you will receive a rich welcome into the everlasting kingdom of our Lord and savior Jesus Christ.

2 Peter 1:5-11

Day 30

Pastor Zhang Rongliang

During the first two months after I was arrested, I was questioned every day. The interrogation was entirely focused on the inner workings of the church. The police wanted to know all the details. Many of the younger investigators were learning things for the first time. The older members were already well versed in the inner workings of the underground House church. They knew me well.

It was hard for them to imagine why anyone would be so gullible as to join the underground House church movement, so they were continually looking for an angle or an ulterior motive. During the first two months I looked for a glimmer of hope that they would be letting me go. No hope came.

"Zhang Rongliang. You are being charged with two counts. You have been informed of the two counts and have been provided with legal counsel. How do you plead?" The judge asked when my day in court finally came.

"I plead not guilty."

From the looks of others in the courtroom, my simple statement did not surprise many people. All of the legal members of the court were prepared to present their case against me. After hearing my case, the judge was not moved.

"Guilty," was the stern verdict. The absoluteness of the moment echoed without fanfare through the courtroom. Soon I was given a piece of paper. I held it up and read it. My crime was spelled out on that paper in black and white. The familiar red star stamp of China with a circle around it glared at me from the bottom of the page to let me know that this was as official as it gets.

At the bottom of the page it read, "For his crimes, Zhang Rongliang is hereby sentenced to eight years."

"Eight years," I said to myself. It was the cycle of my life: in prison or out of prison, on the run or behind bars. It was an emotional roller coaster that I was getting too old for.

I appealed to the middle courts, but it was no use. The Chinese authorities wanted me behind bars, and I was sent to Kaifeng Prison. When I walked in through the gates I thought about China's famous leader who died there, Liu Shaoqi. Liu Shaoqi is China's forgotten president.

Most westerners and even many Chinese have a misinformed view that Mao Zedong was China's one and only national leader during the entirety of his reign.

However, there were about ten years from 1959 to 1969 that China also had a president named Liu Shaoqi. He had a different vision for the future of China and became a political enemy of Mao Zedong. Liu was eventually sent to Kaifeng Prison where he later died. In prison, he was repeatedly beaten and denied medical care for his diabetes. He was eventually found dead on the floor of his cell, covered with diarrhea and vomit. His body was cremated and his family was not informed of his death until three years later.

"Is this the place where I will die?" I asked myself. Like Liu Shaoqi, I was sentenced to Kaifeng Prison as a political prisoner. My health had been deteriorating and I was not sure how I would handle the hard labor. I had a sinking feeling that I would never leave that place alive.

I was shown to my cell in the prison. I tried to remain cheerful, but was not able to conjure up the joy to break a smile. Eight years seemed like a death sentence and I was certain that I would never see the other side of the prison walls. When I walked around and was introduced to my work responsibilities, I was even more convinced of my fate. My old body would not be able to handle the hard labor much longer. I could see strong young men strain as they worked the presses in a crude factory environment. Some were working on furniture coverings, pushing and pulling heavy material and using the core strength of their bodies. Bundles of material were being hoisted upon the shoulders of young men who were only about one-third my age. I shook my head at the sight of it.

"I can't," I said to myself. "I can't do this." I was

mentally knocked down before I even started.

"This is surely where I will die. This sweatshop will be the end of me," I thought, but the Lord spoke to my heart in that low moment.

"No. I will not leave you. I will be with you. I will lead you out of here."

The sweet sound of my Father's voice bounced through my soul with warm vibrancy. This was the voice of the Father who had carried me during the darkest days that I have ever experienced in a prison cell. When I was tied up and tortured, His voice gave me strength. When I was hungry and laying on the cold concrete floor without a blanket, His love brought me warmth. The words of the Father brought me hope, not just because they were comforting, but because they were familiar to me. The familiarity of my Father's voice that has sustained me over the years brought nourishment for my soul. With this newfound hope, I knew that I would make it.

Seven years later, in 2011, when I received my release papers and began to walk out of the prison, I turned and looked back at the prison and could see many of my friends waving to me. Some of them had grabbed their towels and were using them to wave with. Some of them had even run back to their cells to grab sheets off of their beds and then had run back to the windows to wave them at me.

I couldn't help but feel love and compassion for those whom I was leaving behind. The Spirit of the Lord came upon me and I could hear Him say, "Just as you sent men and women to preach the Gospel to the far flung provinces of China, Asia, and the Middle East, so have I sent you to preach the Gospel to the prisoners of Kaifeng."

The words of the Lord stunned me. It was no easier for the young missionaries who went into foreign lands to preach the Gospel to the lost than it was for me to be sent to Kaifeng Prison. I was never alone. God was with me every step of the way, providing me with comfort and power. Being in Kaifeng was not about me at all. It was about God.

I am crucified with Christ and it is no longer I who live, but He who lives in me. I had kept thinking of my journey as a personal trial to make me stronger and closer to God. I saw the trials of prison as God's way of bringing me closer to Him. Standing there and watching all of those enthusiastic young men waving at me as I walked out, I realized how selfish those thoughts had been. It was not about me at all—it was about my fellow prisoners and, ultimately, it was about God's glory. It was about God's love becoming known to all men for His glory alone, even those at Kaifeng Prison.

Even though my trial was not easy, I would not trade those seven years for anything. I think of Shadrach, Meshach, and Abednego as they were in the fiery furnace. The furnace was hot, but they were not burned up. Not only were they not burned up, but they were walking around joyfully in the midst of the flames! With those thoughts echoing in my mind, I turned and walked out of Kaifeng Prison.

THINK ABOUT IT

Men and women all around the world today are preaching the Gospel of Jesus Christ in the hardest-to-reach areas on earth. They have left the comfort of their homes, the security of their jobs, the investments of their youth to take the Good News into the most inhospitable areas known to mankind.

What have you done for the Kingdom of God? Better yet – what are you going to do?

SCRIPTURE READING

Love should be shown without pretending. Hate evil, and hold on to what is good. Love each other like the members of your family. Be the best at showing honor to each other. Don't hesitate to be enthusiastic—be on fire in the Spirit as you serve the Lord! Be happy in your hope, stand your ground when you're in trouble, and devote yourselves to prayer. Contribute to the needs of God's people, and welcome strangers into your home. Bless people who harass you—bless and don't curse them. Be happy with those who are happy, and cry with those who are crying. Consider everyone as equal, and don't think that you're better than anyone else. Instead, associate with people who have no status. Don't think that you're so smart. Don't pay back anyone for their evil actions with evil actions, but show respect for what everyone else believes is good.

If possible, to the best of your ability, live at peace with all people. Don't try to get revenge for yourselves, my dear friends, but leave room for God's wrath. It is written, Revenge belongs to me; I will pay it back, says the Lord. Instead, If your enemy is hungry, feed him; if he is thirsty, give him a drink. By doing this, you will pile burning coals of fire upon his head. Don't be defeated by evil, but defeat evil with good.

Romans 12:9-21

CONCLUSION

Do you remember being in High School and receiving your yearbook near the end of the school year?

What is the first thing you did after receiving your copy? If you are like most people, you sat down somewhere nearby and quickly thumbed through the yearbook to see what pictures it contained of you. There was plenty of information compiled in the book about your school and your friends, but your first goal was to find pictures of yourself.

Once you found them, you may even have marked them and made a mental note of whether they were silly or acceptable.

We often look at the Bible in the same way. We like to thumb through it and find all of the verses and stories that remind us of ourselves. We want to know how the Bible relates to our own lives. Essentially we are looking for our own picture in the Bible.

If we only see every passage in the Bible in how it relates to us, then we will miss out on many other things that the Bible has to say to us. The Bible is not just a guide to understand how you relate to God, but it is also a guide for how we should relate to one another.

The stories in the Bible are not imaginary fairy tales, but real accounts from history that not only tell us about God, but tell us about the suffering of man in his search for God. It is a collection of the real life sufferings of our forefathers throughout time. The Bible uniquely captures the world through their eyes, in their culture, during their time. It is a time capsule preserving the sufferings, victories, mistakes, and triumphs of mankind.

Learning to empathize and identify with the suffering of others will actually tell us more about who we are individually.

Such stories did not end with the completion of the Bible, but continue today in an un-canonized form. The Jehovah of the Bible is a living God who continues to be involved in the lives of His people every day.

Stories that echo the goodness of God continue to be told around the world and since China is the most populated country on earth, its believers have many stories to share. China's home churches may not look like the traditional church buildings that dot the landscapes of Europe and America, but they are real and their stories are powerful.

Even though Jesus was a carpenter, He never once built a church building. He was more invested in people and in glorifying His Father. He is more invested in you than in your accomplishments. He wants a closer relationship with you.

It has been said that if Jesus wanted to reach cats, He would have become a kitten. If He wanted to reach cows, He would have become a calf, but He wanted to reach man so He came to the earth as an innocent child. He came and invested in others and suffered with man.

Jesus came to us to reach us. If we want to reach the world, we will have to follow in Jesus' footsteps, the way the Chinese have, and go to where the world is.

It does our souls well to be inspired by these stories from the battlefield. May we take them to heart.

"Look among the nations and see; wonder and be astounded. For I am doing a work in your days that you would not believe if told."

Habakkuk 1:5

BACK TO
归耶路撒冷
JERUSALEM

For more information and resources on the
Chinese House church and the Back to Jerusalem
missionary movement go to :

www.backtoJerusalem.com

Or you can contact :

Back to Jerusalem
277 Lower Airport Rd,
Lumberton, MS 39455

Phone: (601) 543-5683
Email: info@backtojerusalem.com